THE
JOHN F. KENNEDYS

BY

MARK SHAW

A FAMILY ALBUM

FARRAR, STRAUS

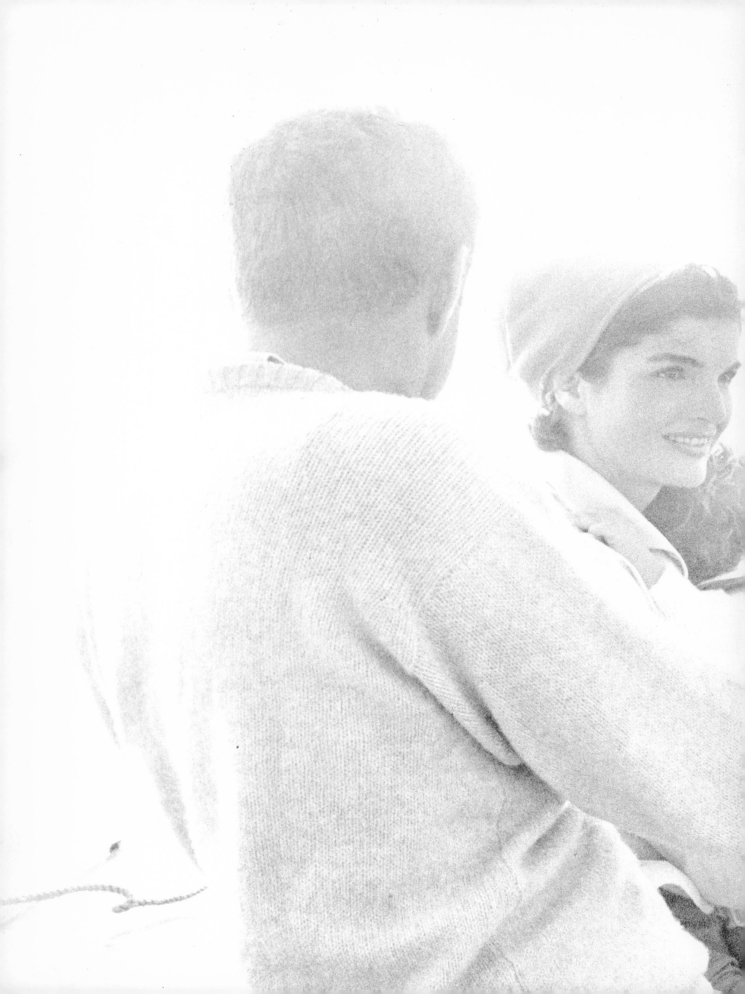

THE
JOHN F. KENNEDYS

BY
MARK SHAW

DESIGNED BY ROBERT CATO

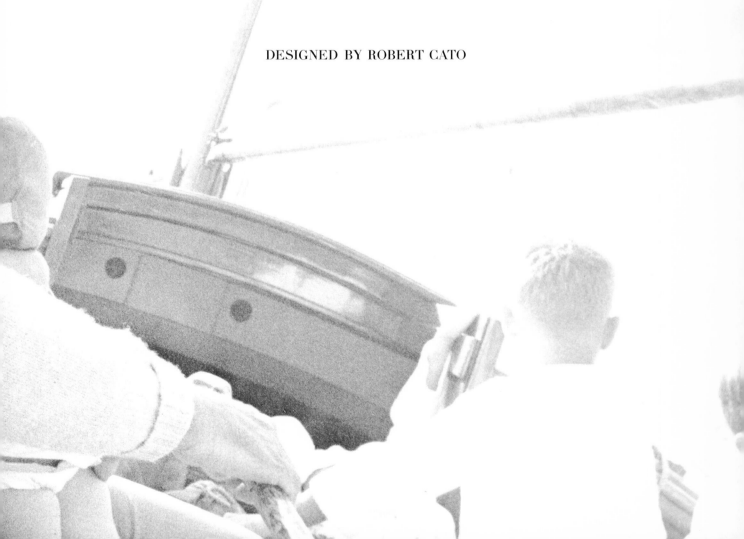

Copyright © 1959, 1960, 1961, 1962, 1963, 1964 by Mark Shaw
Library of Congress catalog card number 64-16278
Fifth Printing, 1964

Published simultaneously in Canada by Ambassador Books, Ltd., Toronto.
Printed in the United States of America by
Sanders Printing Corporation, New York, in Santaglio II.

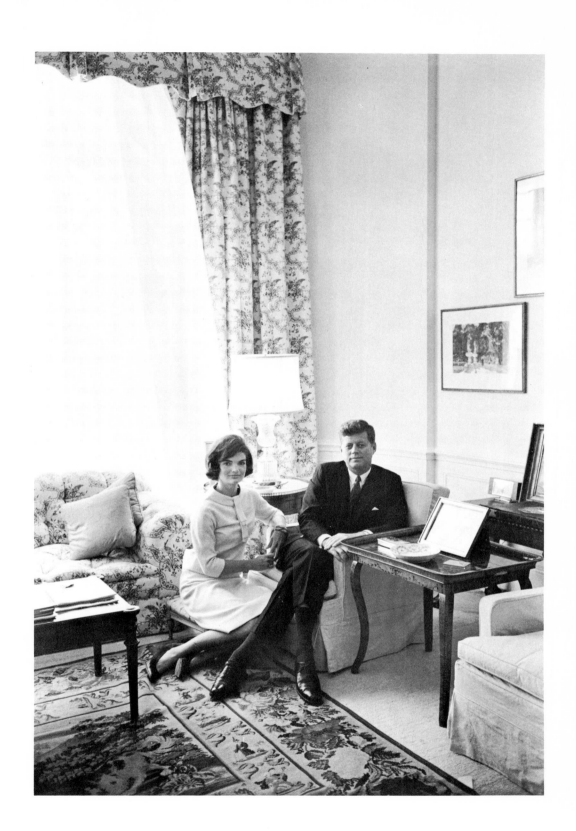

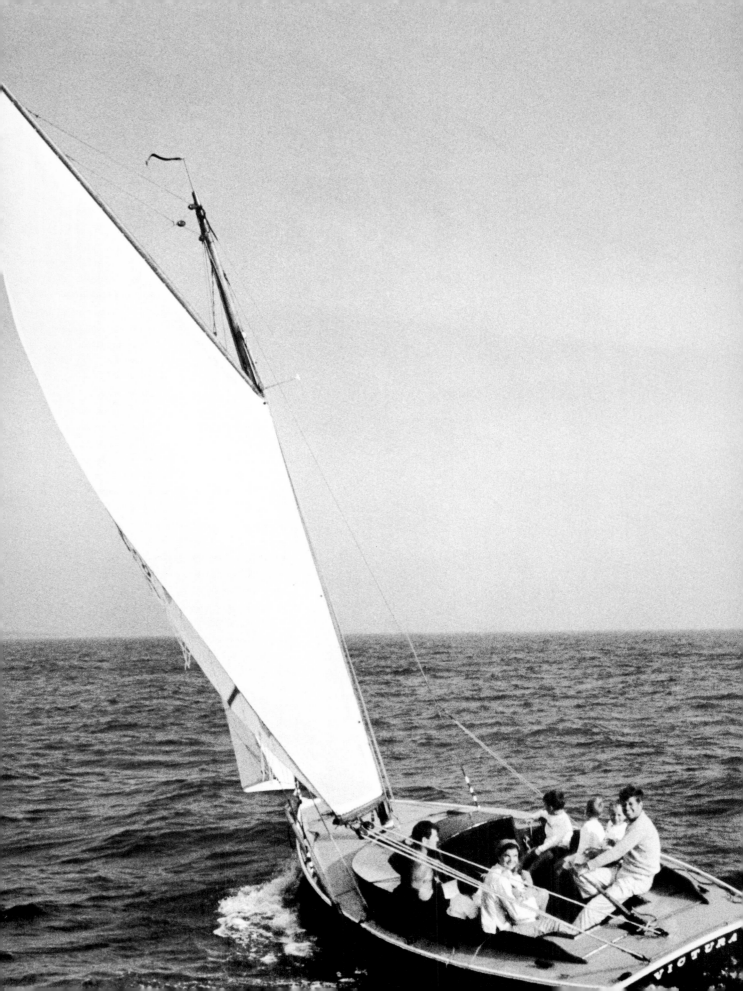

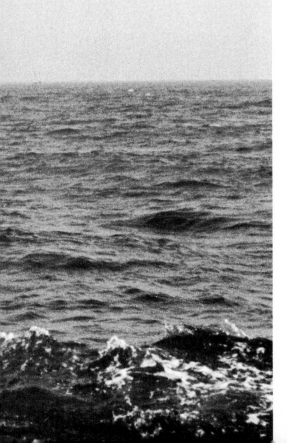

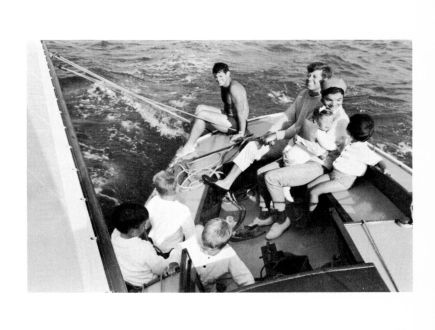

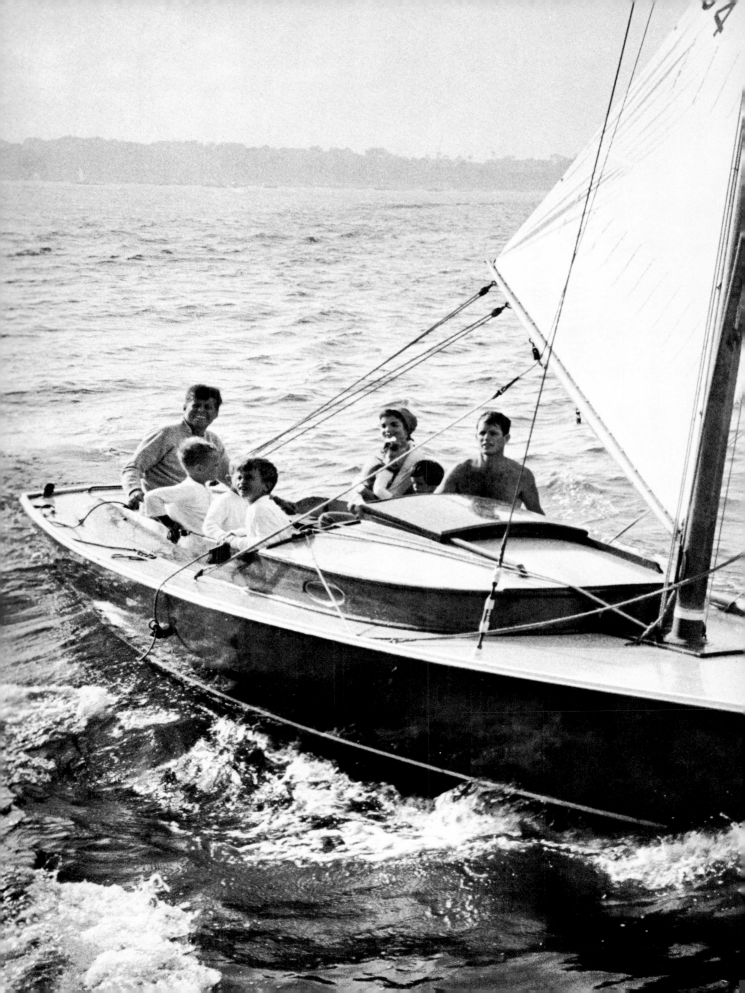

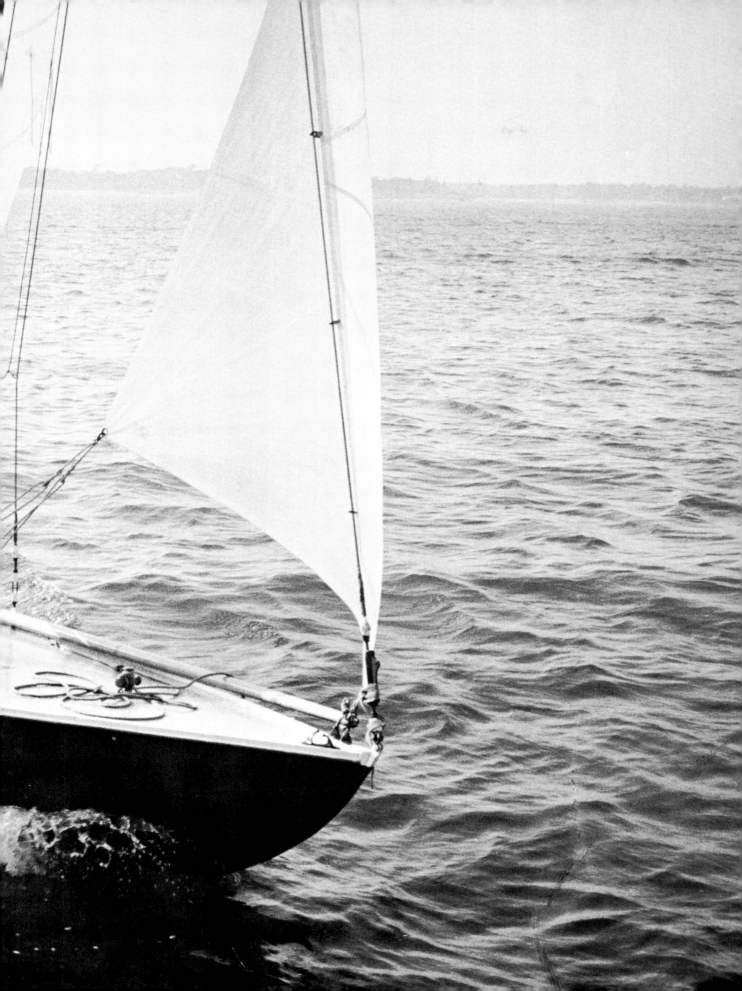

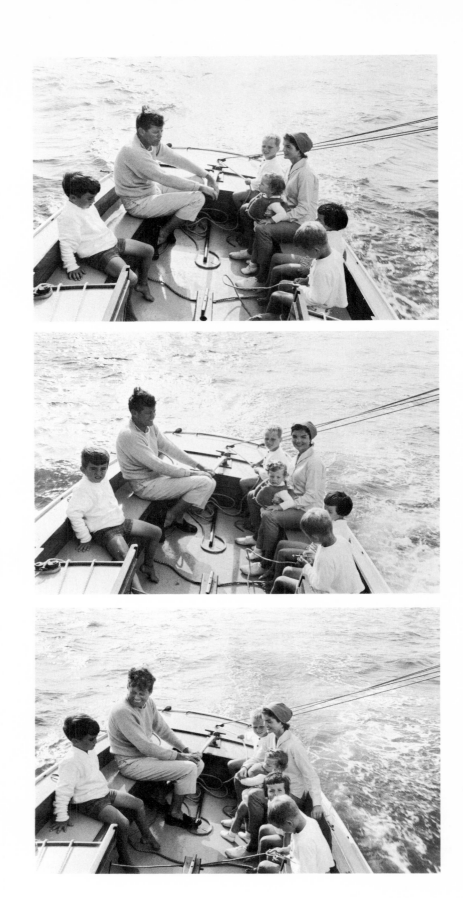

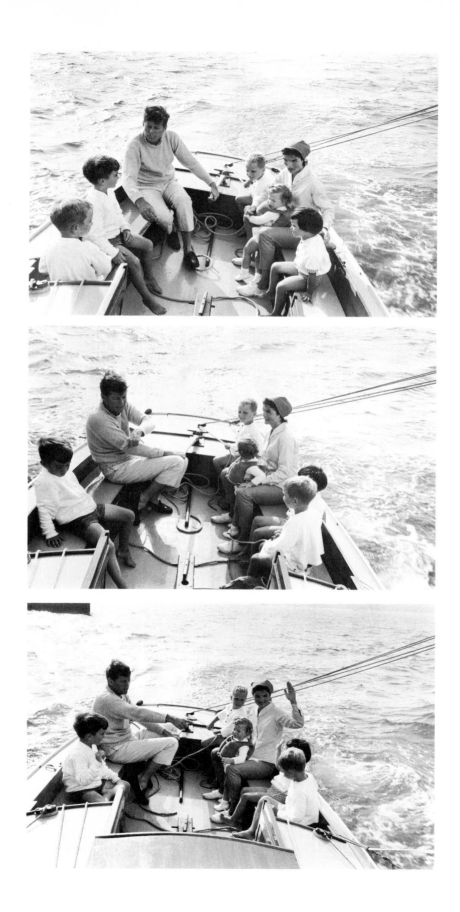

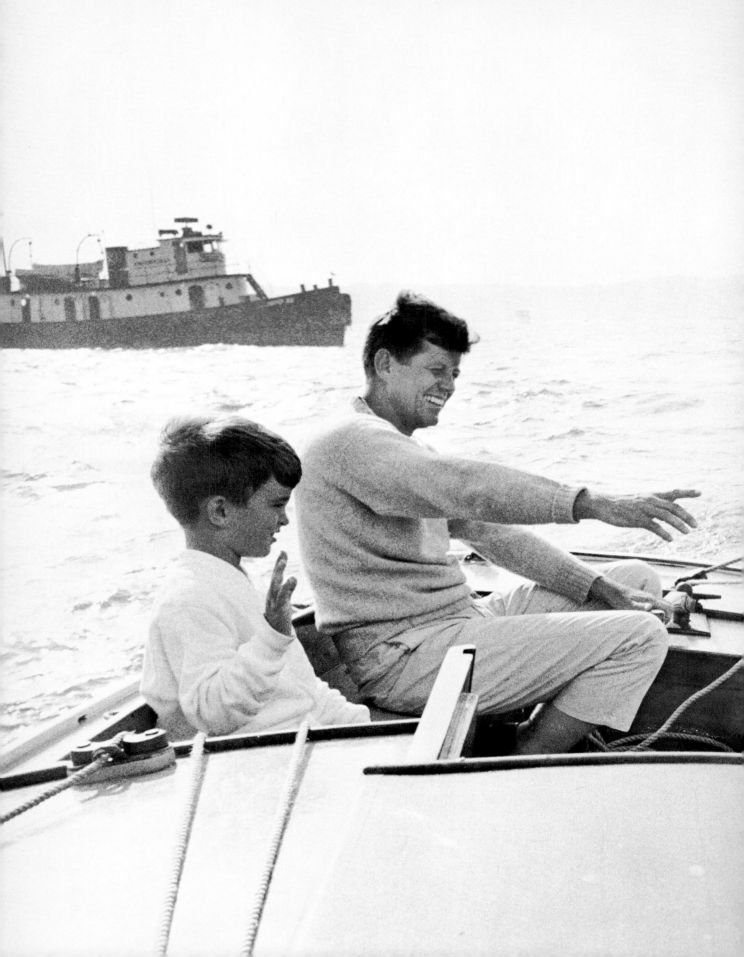

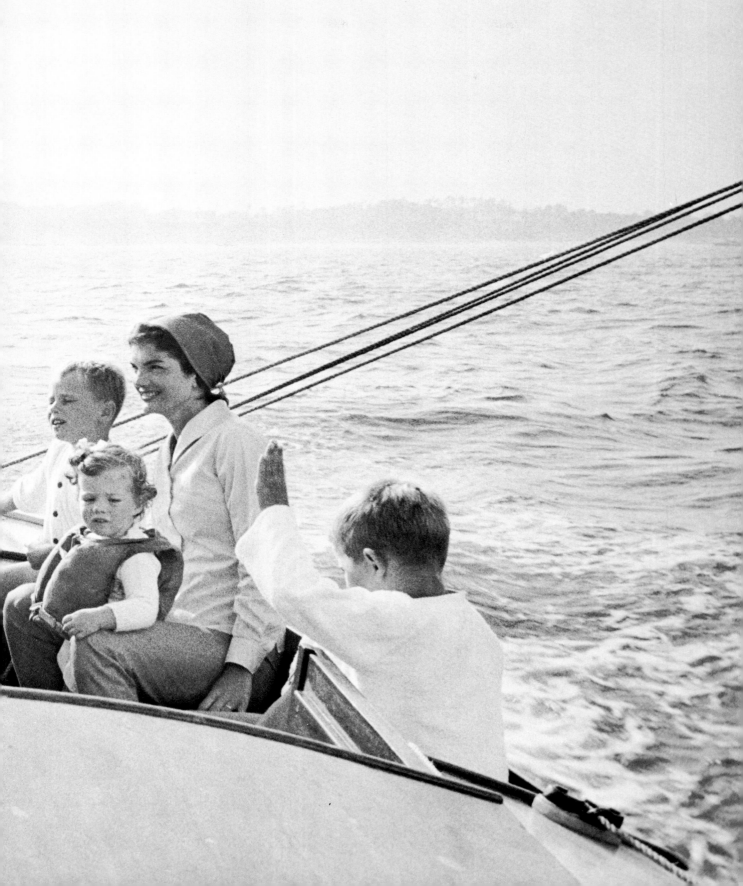

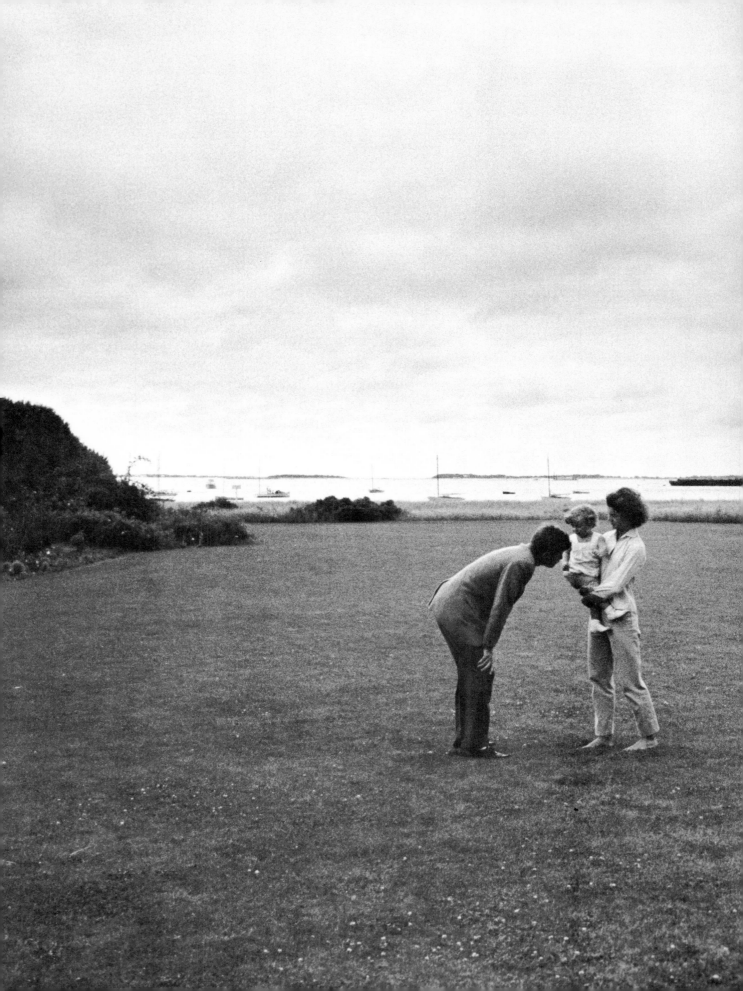

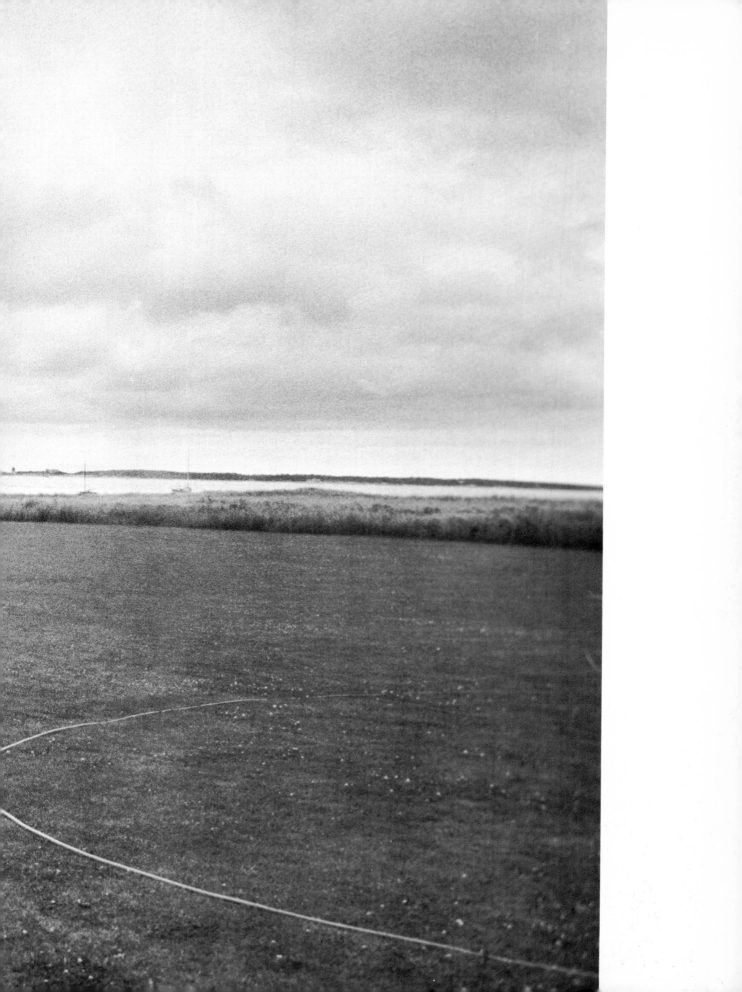

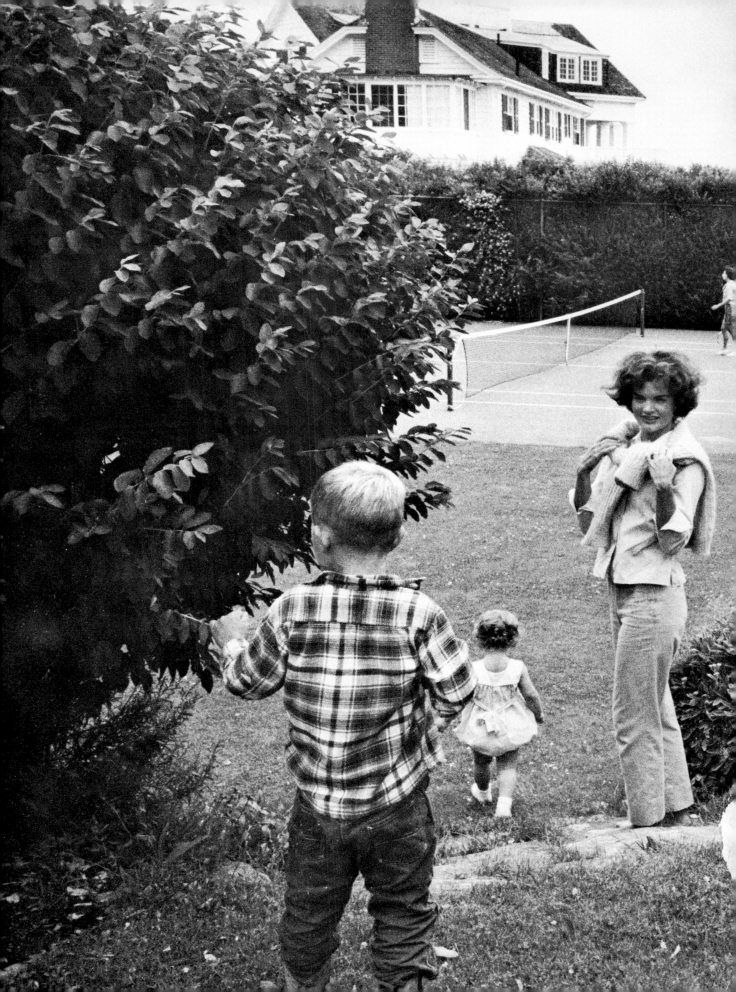

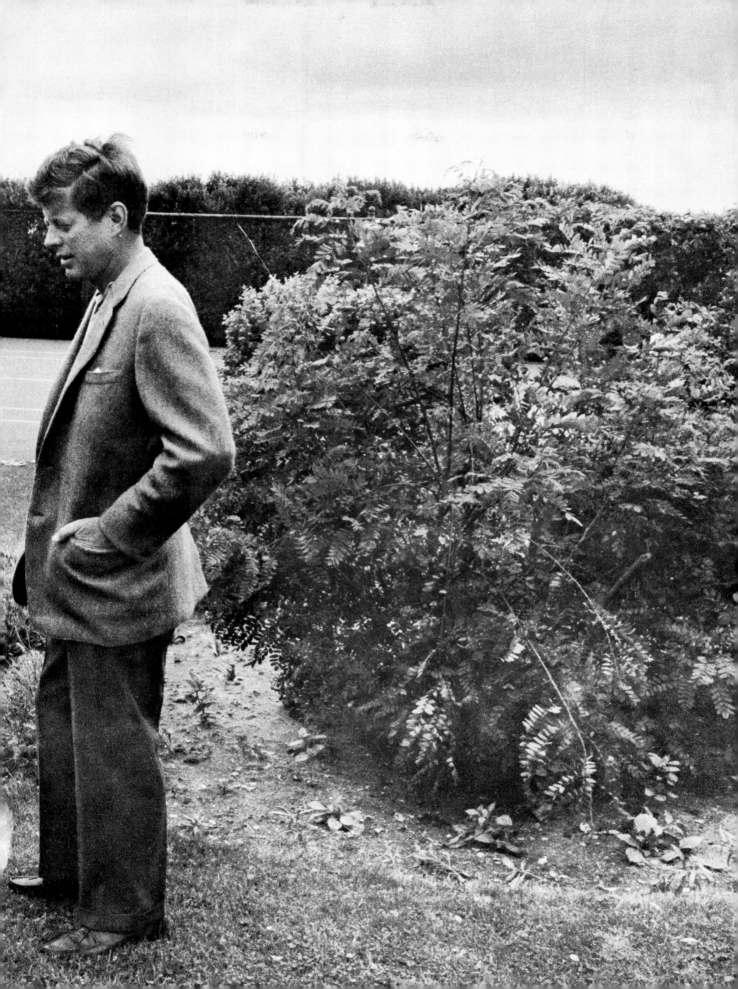

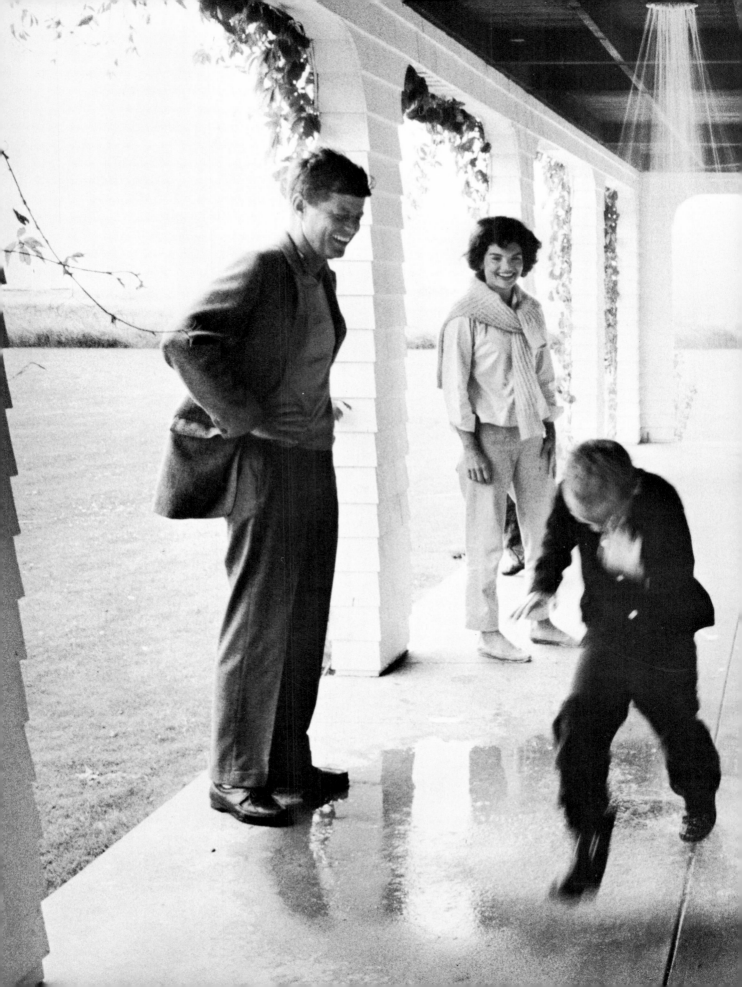

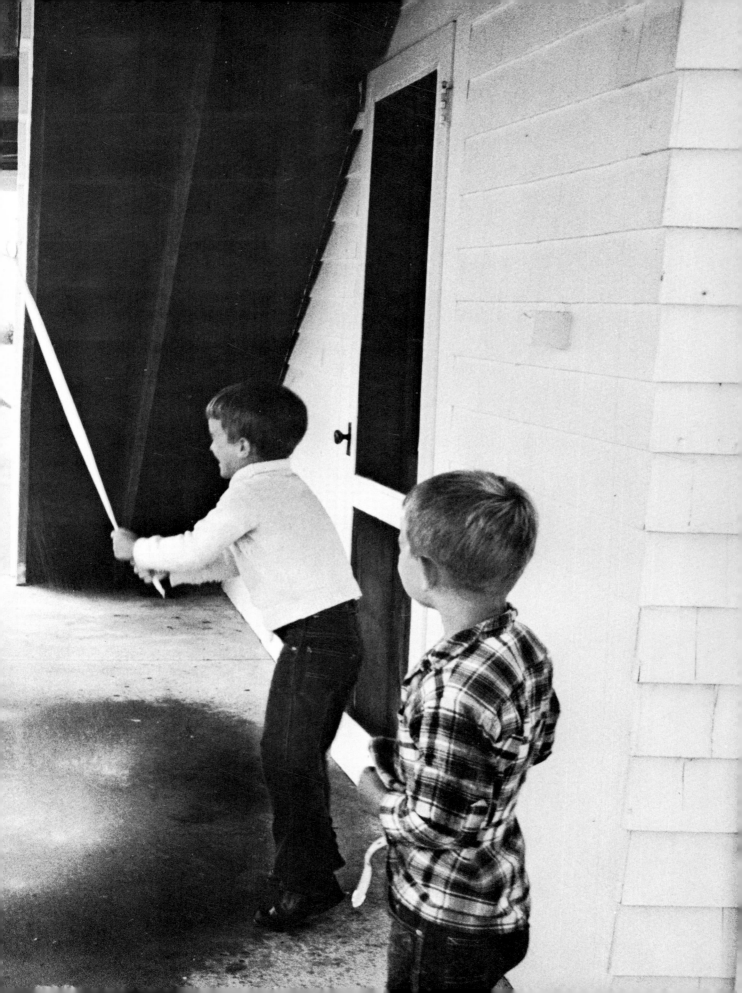

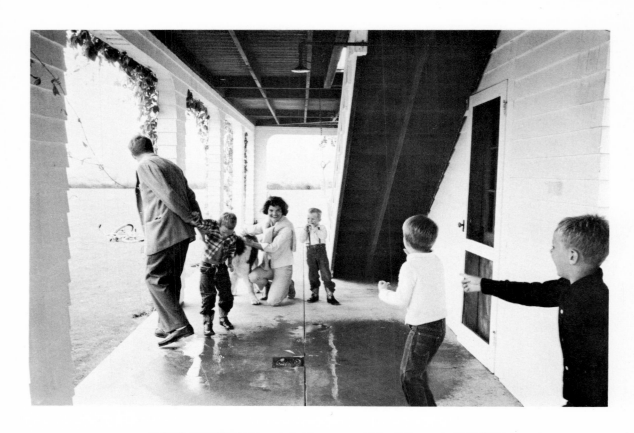

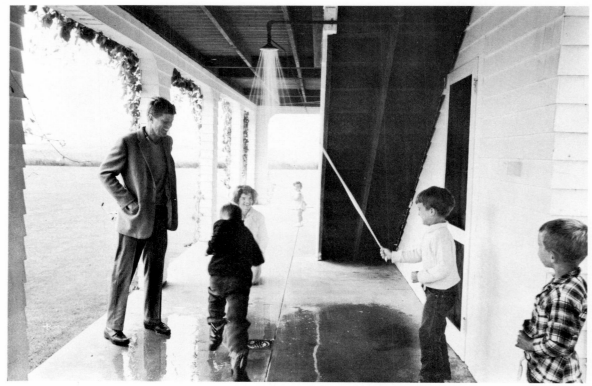

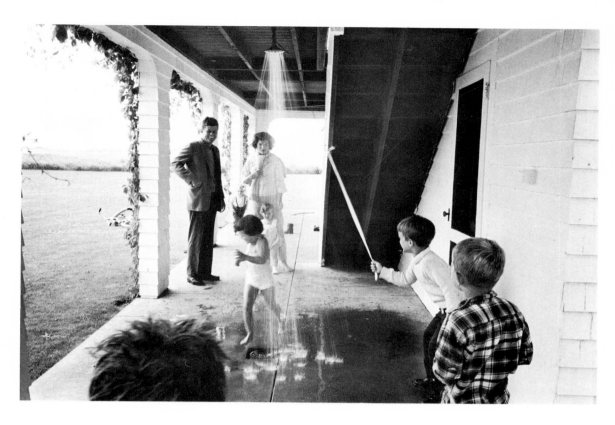

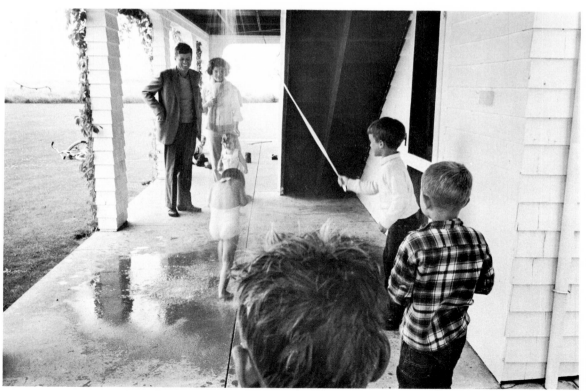

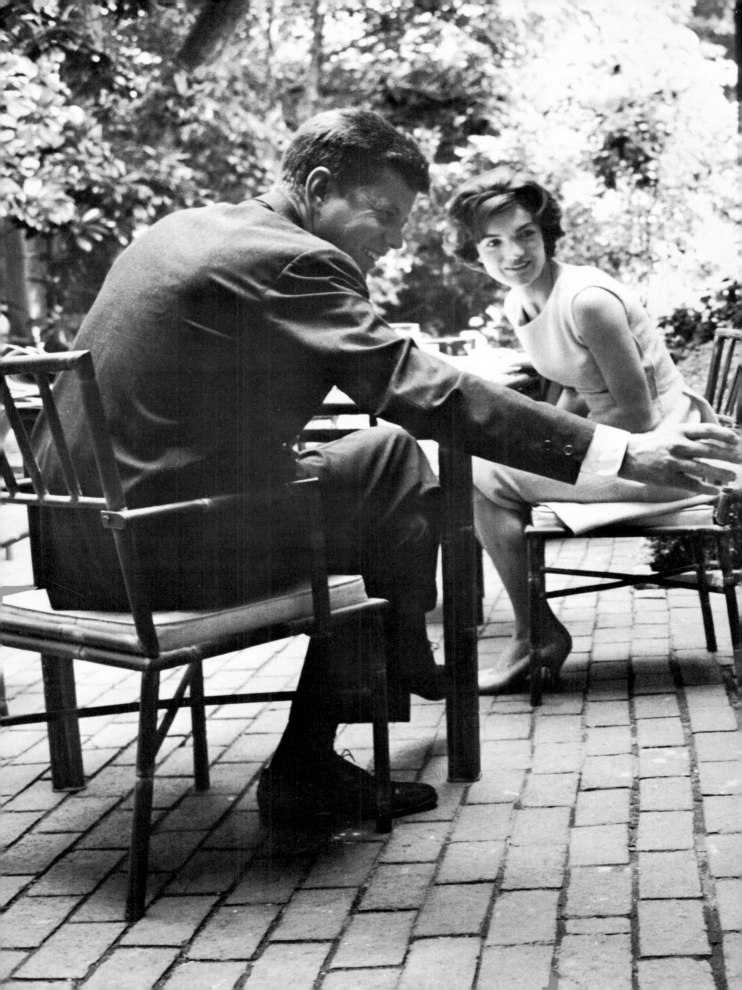

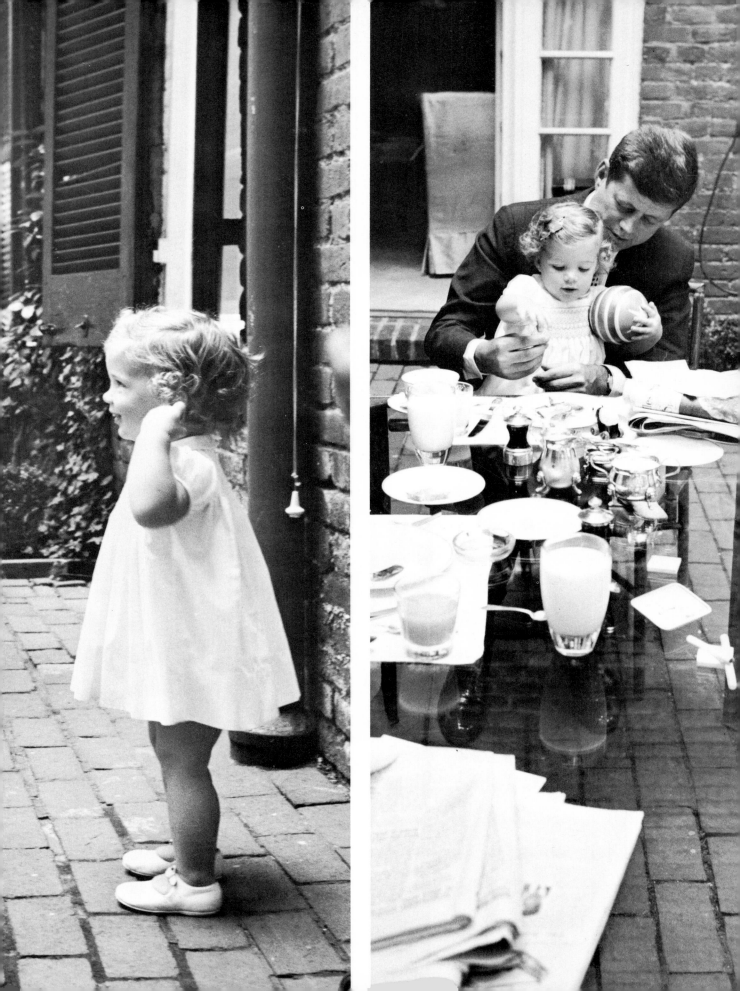

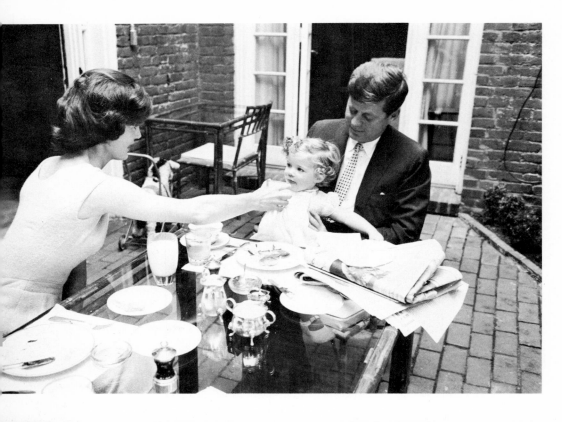

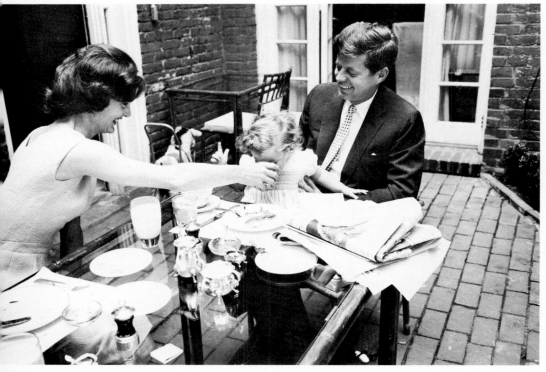

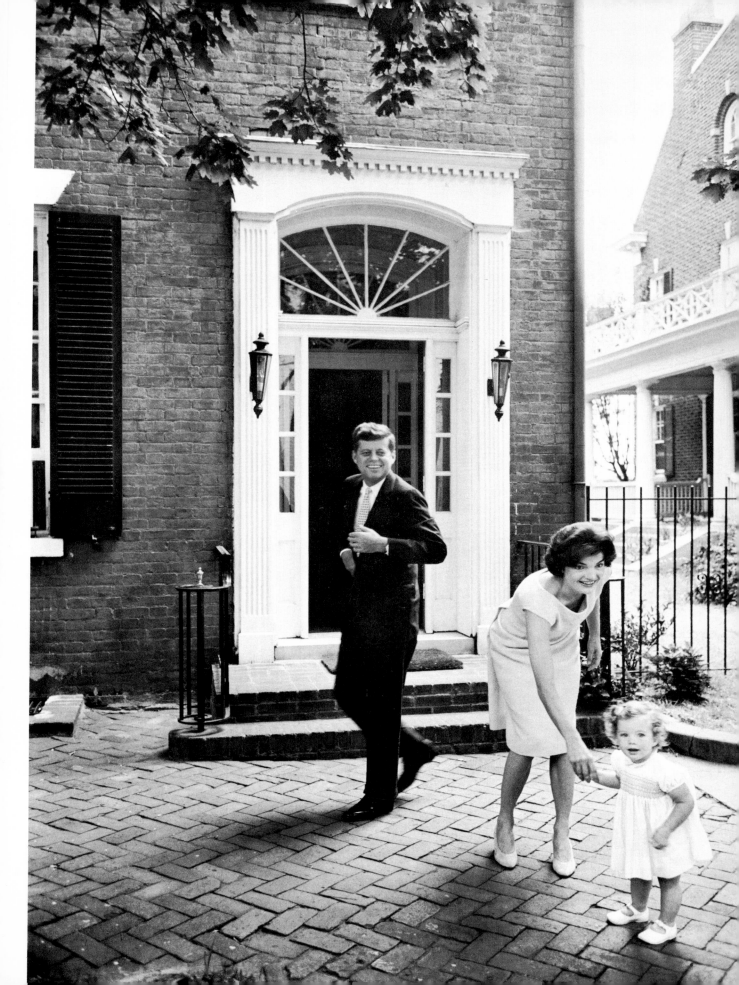

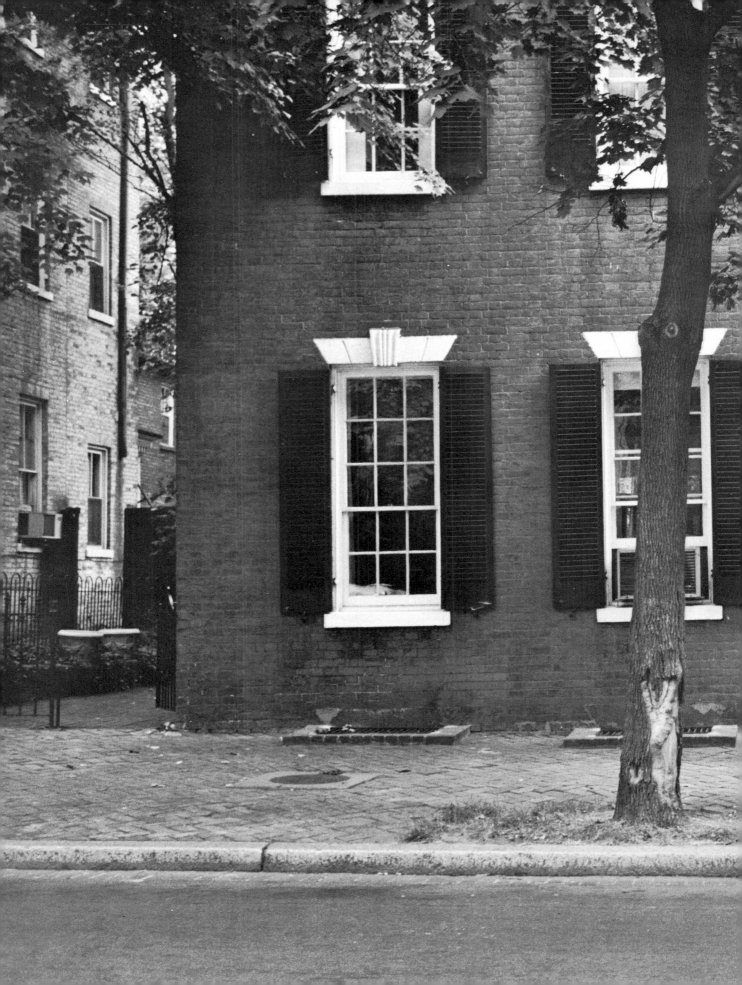

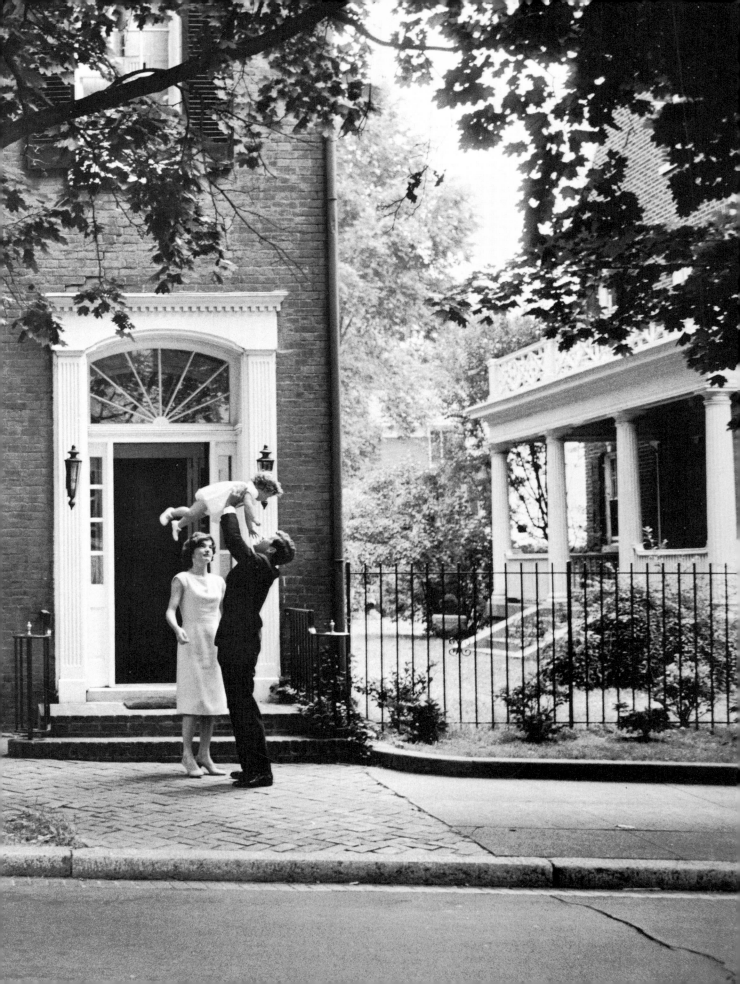

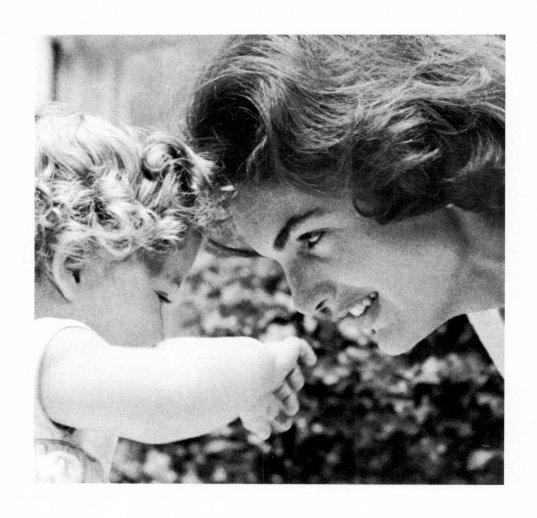

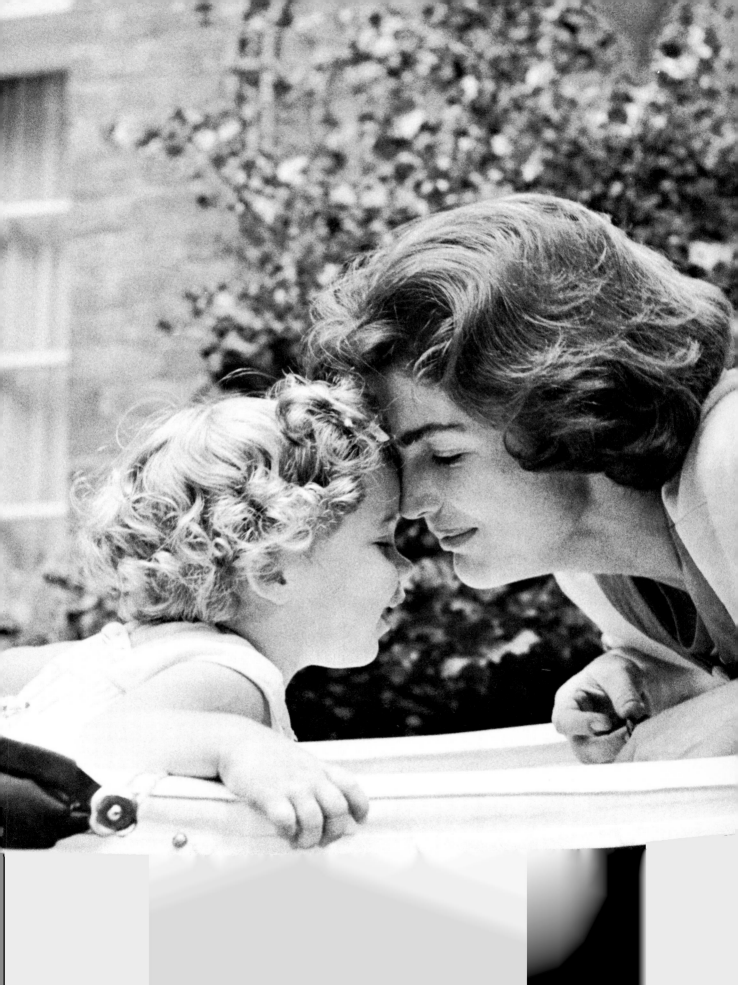

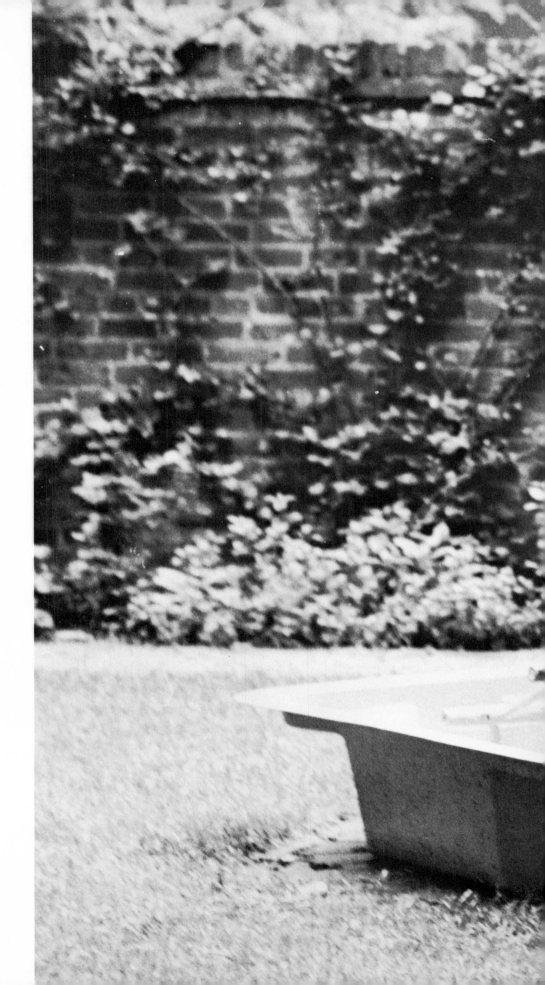

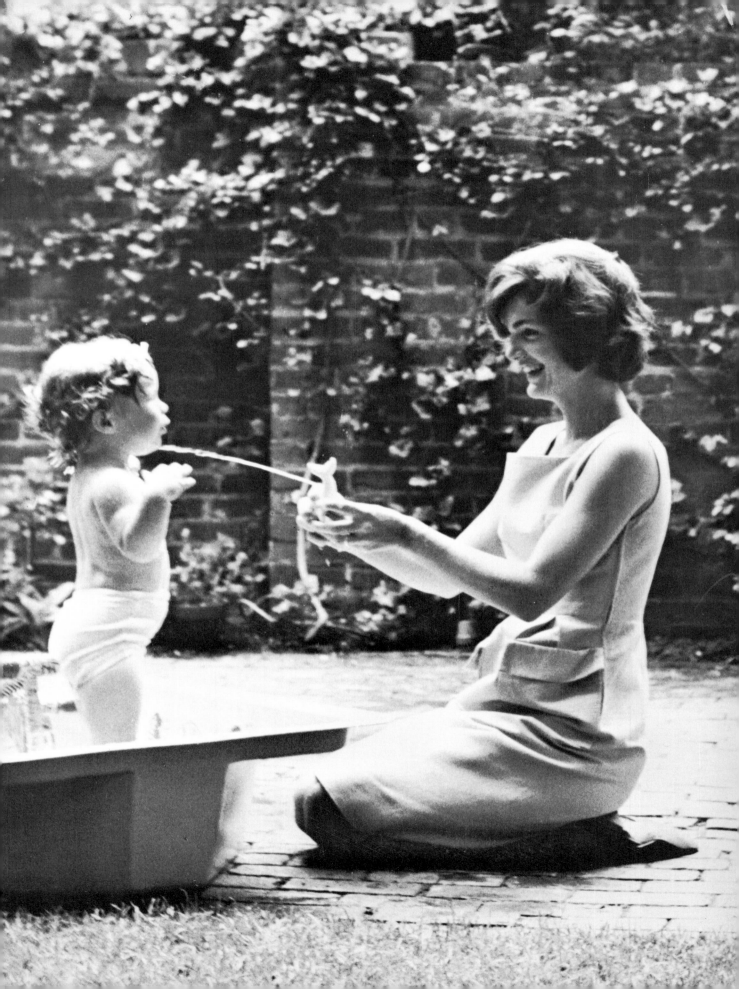

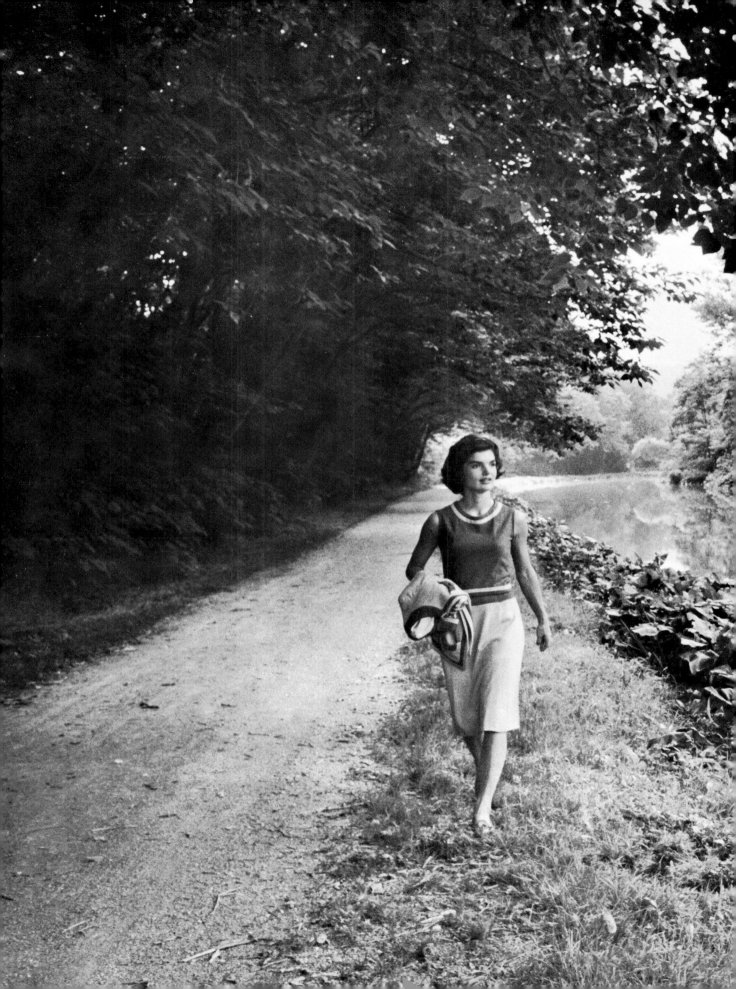

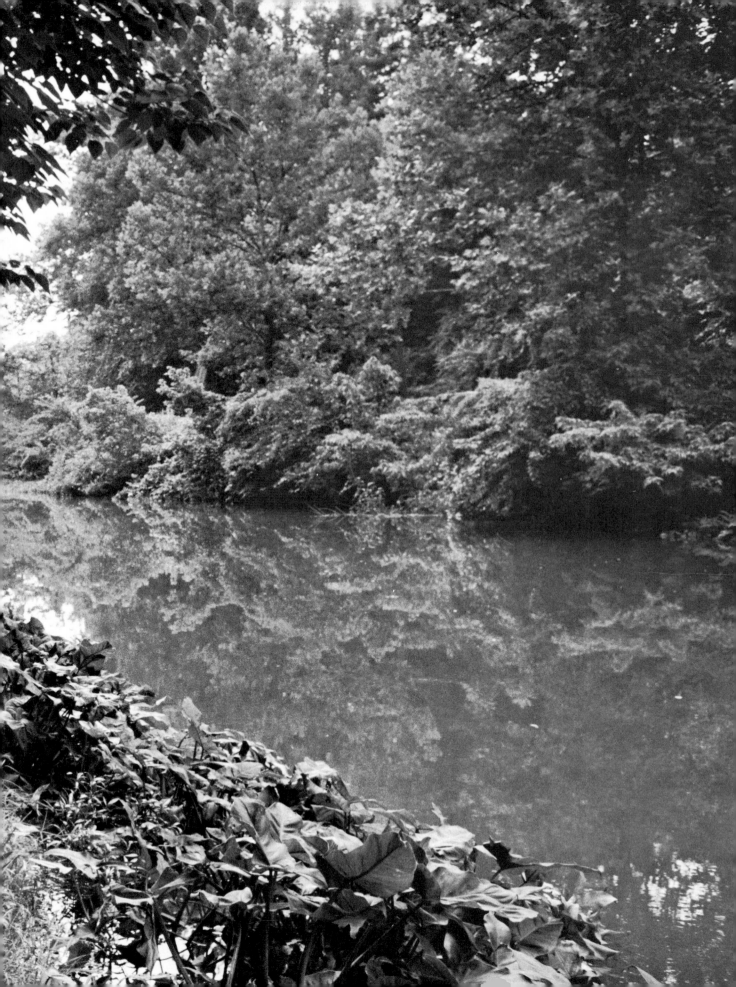

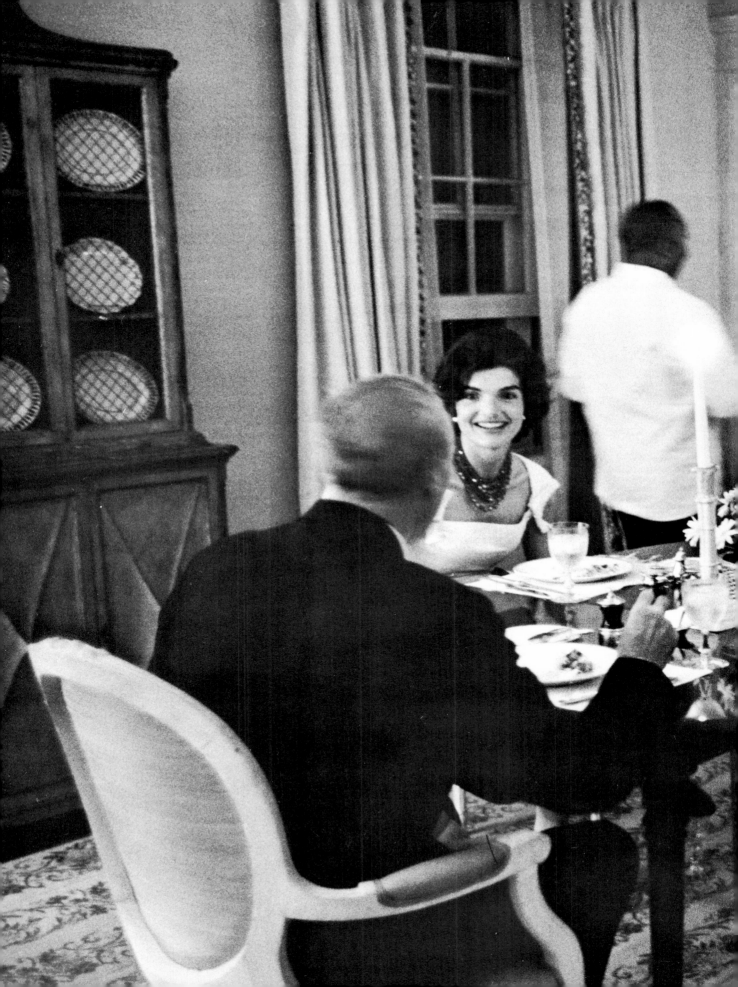

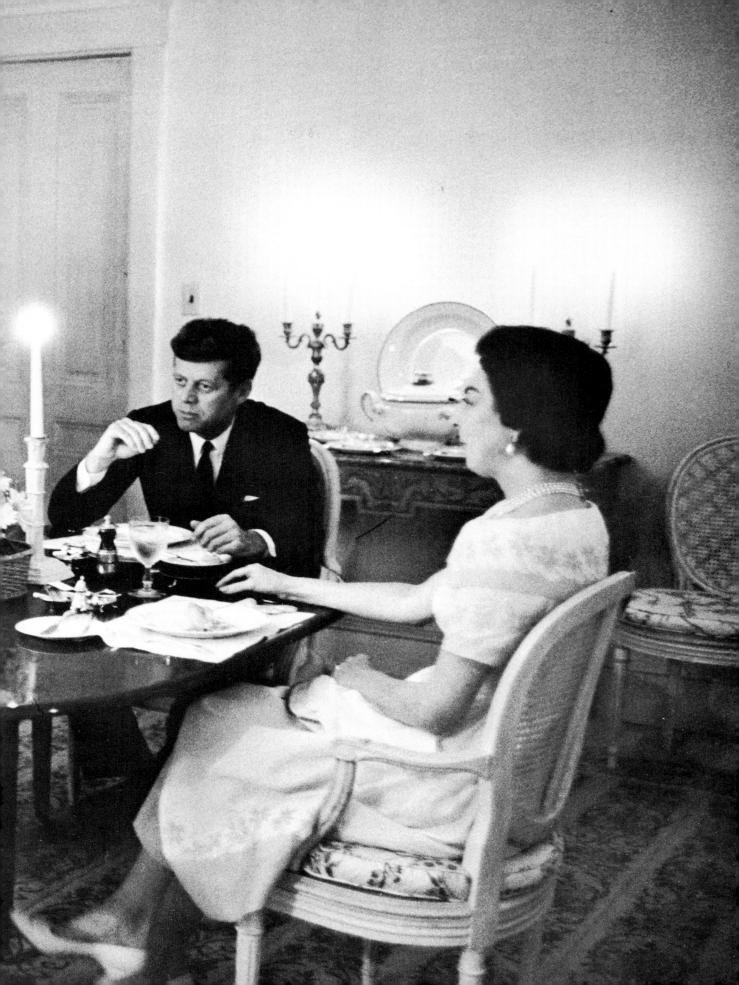

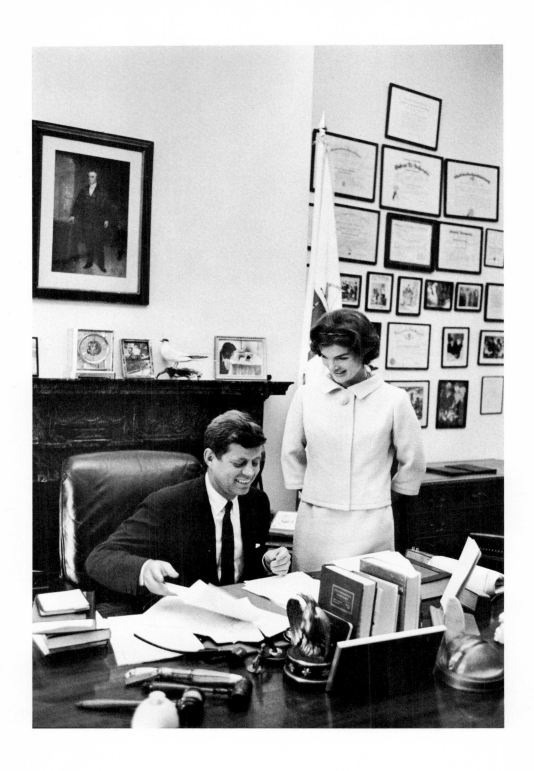

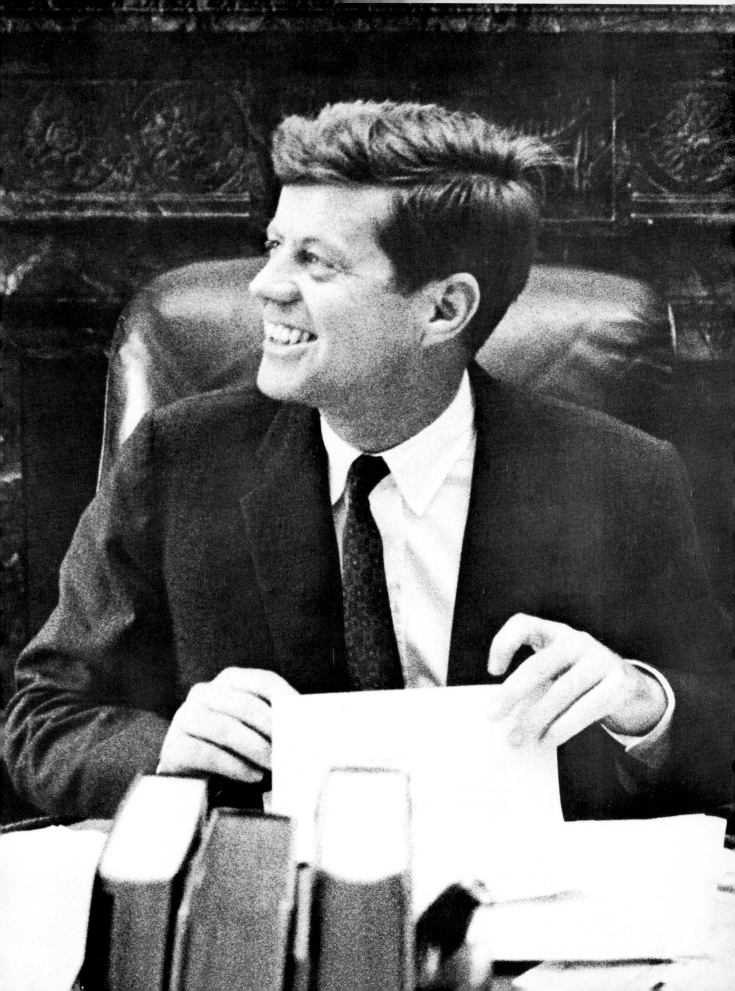

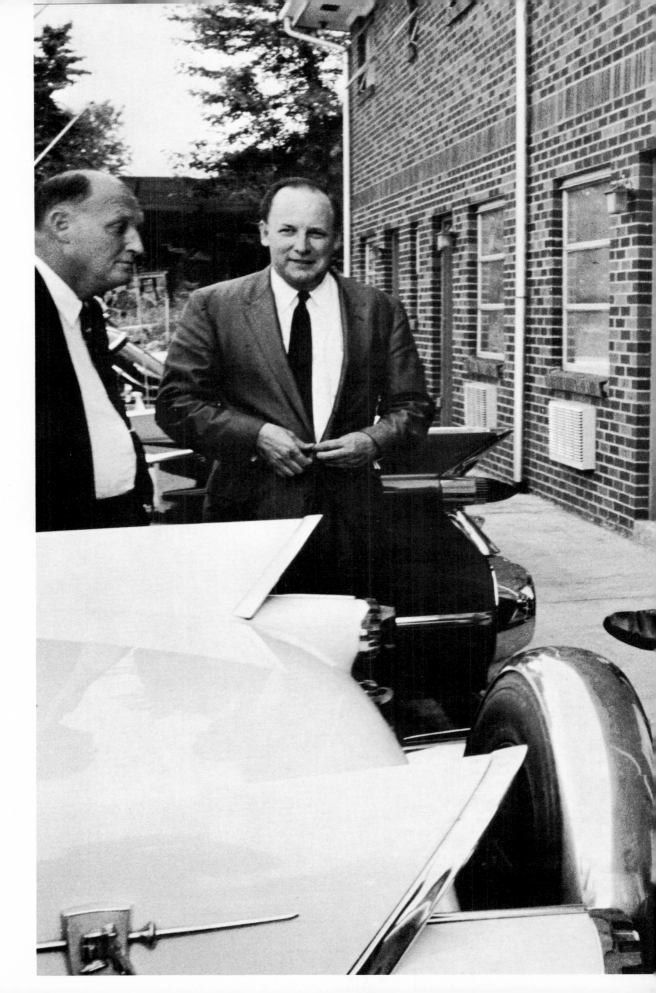

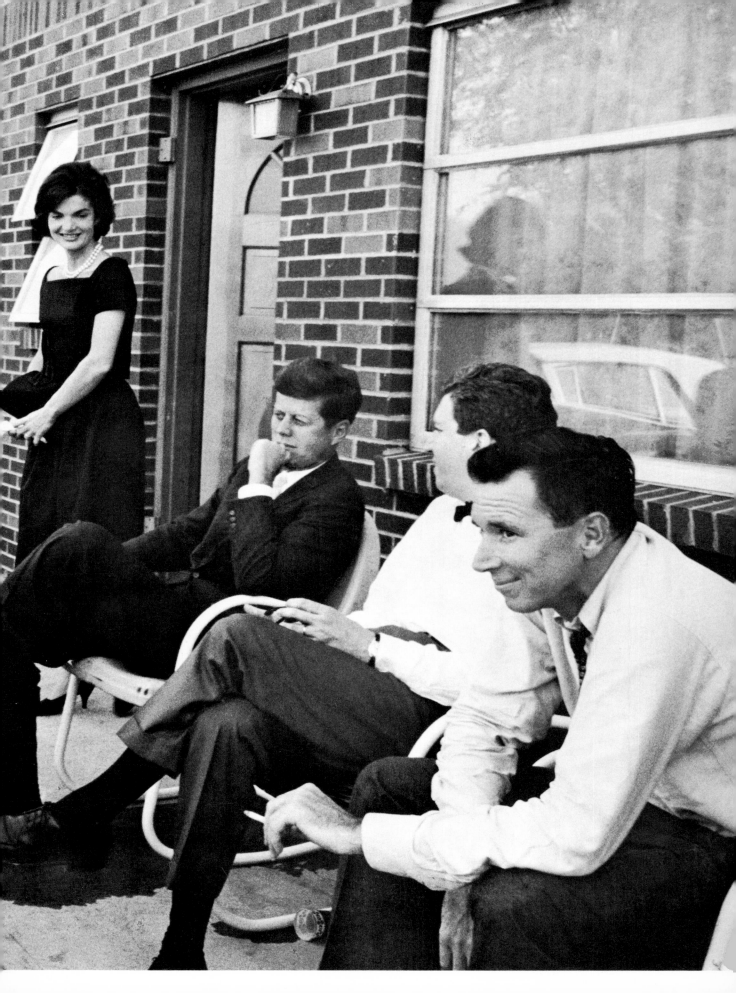

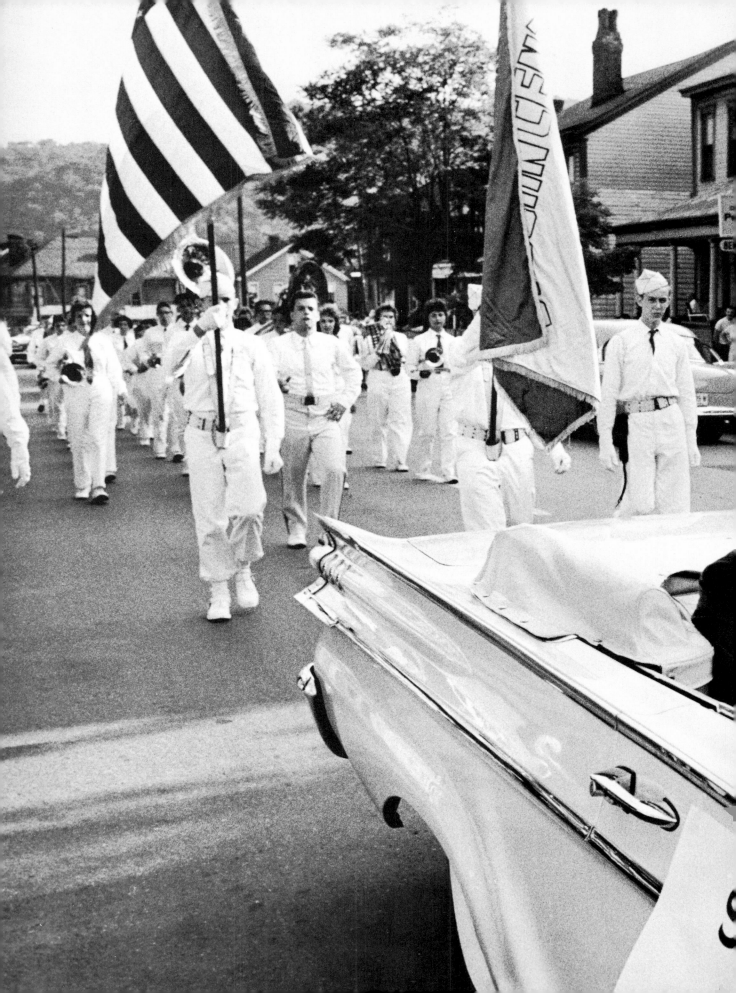

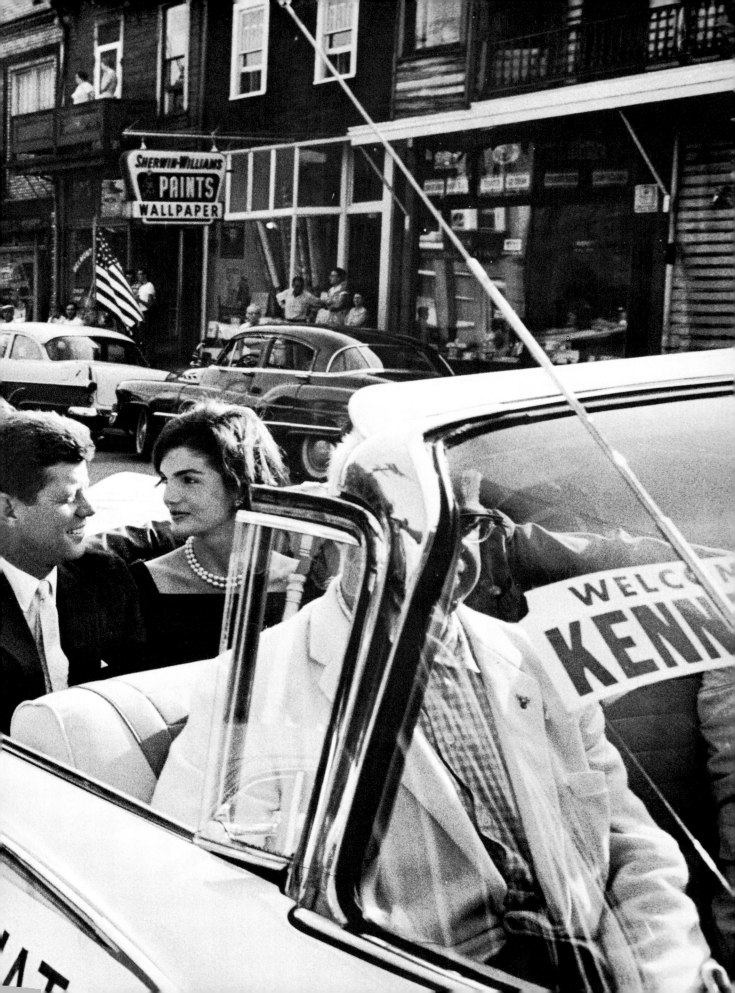

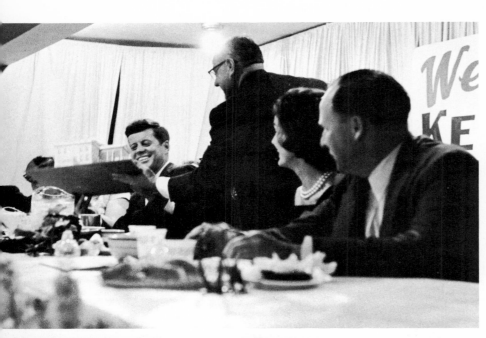

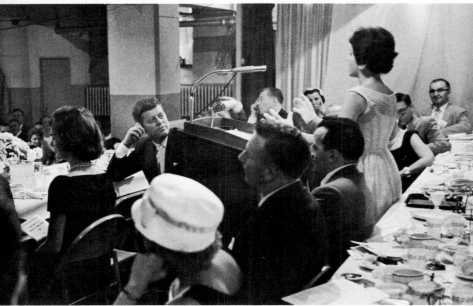

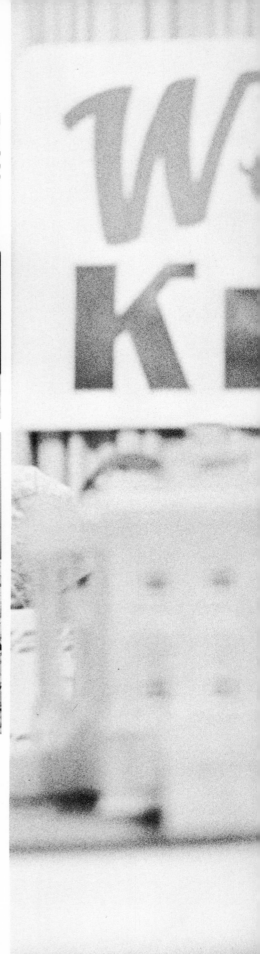

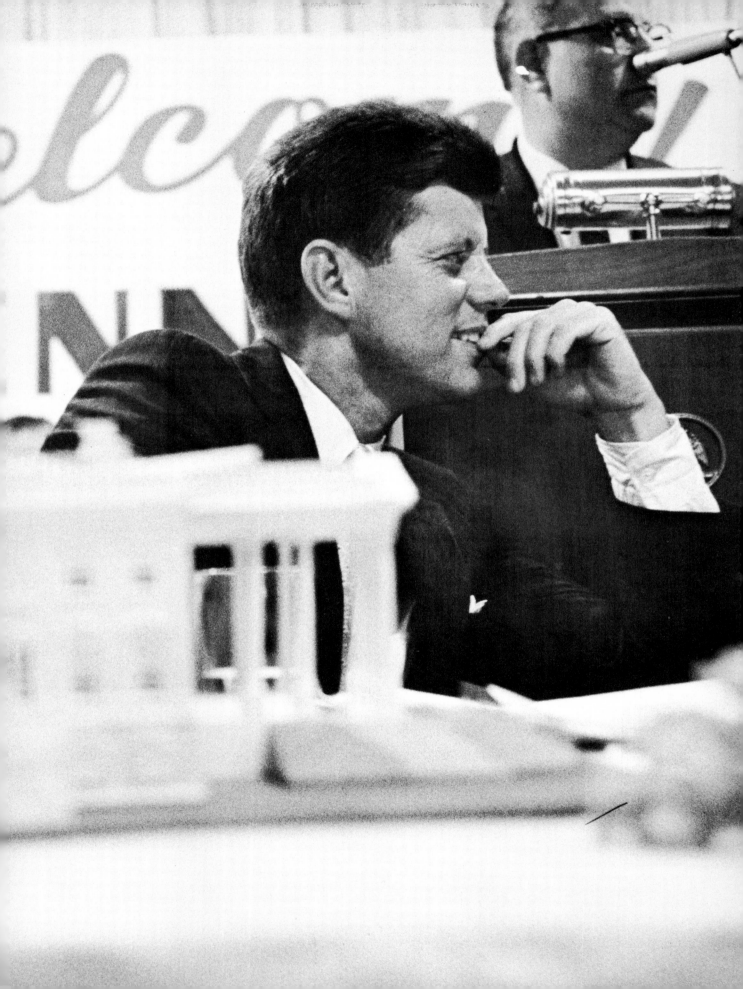

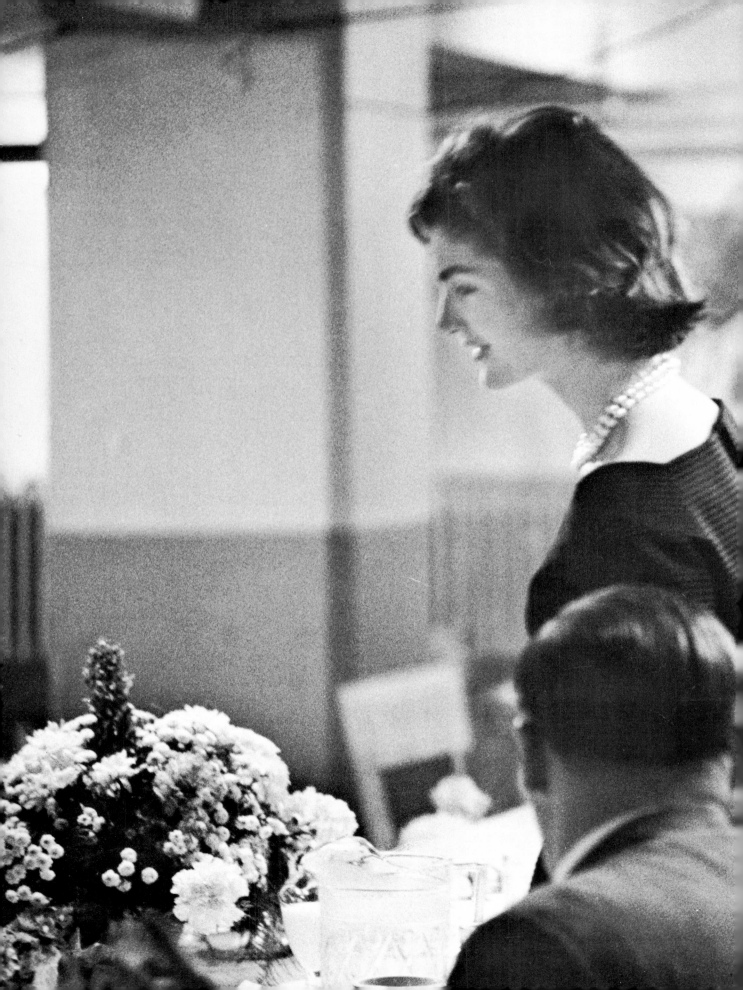

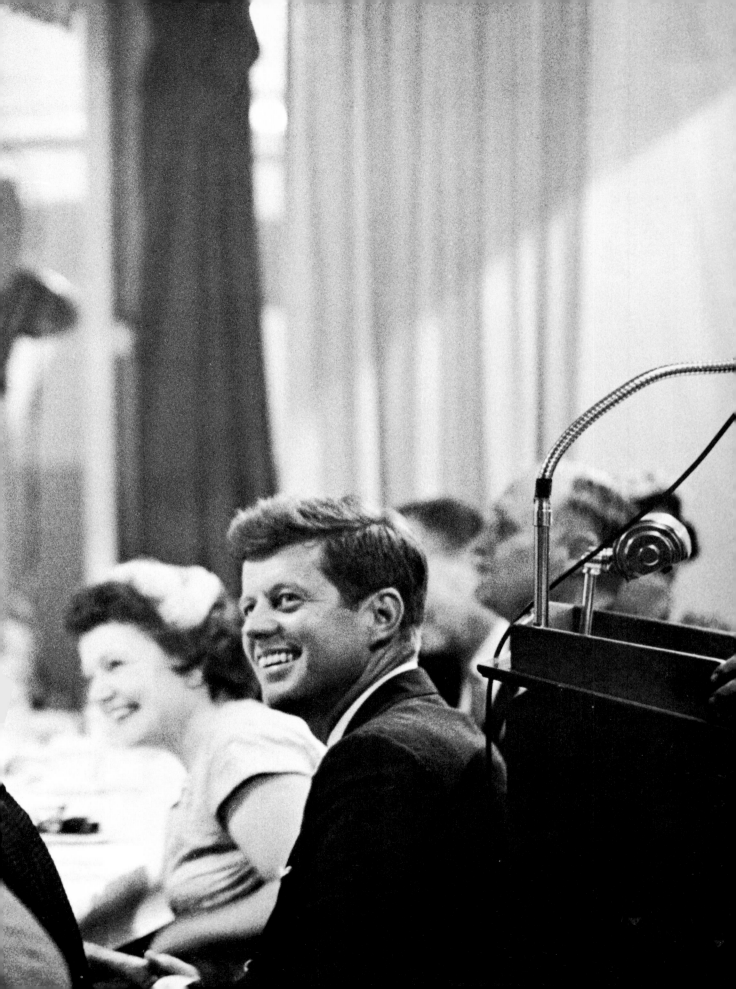

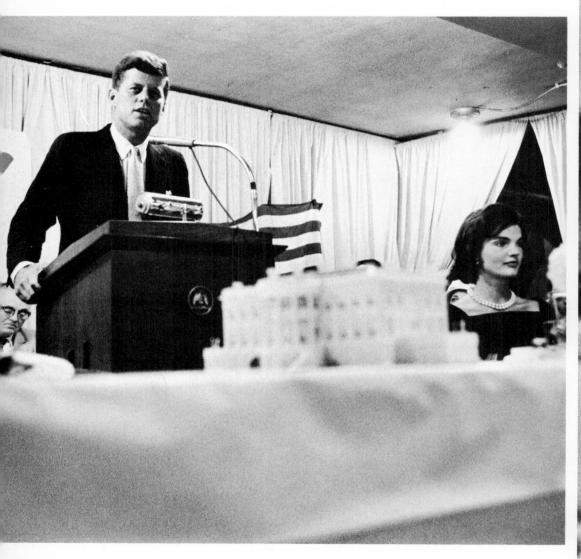

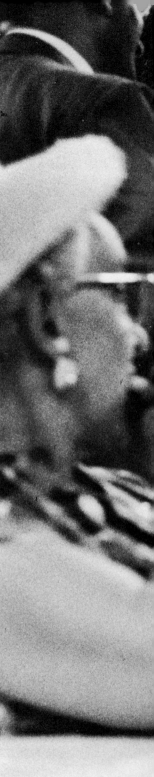

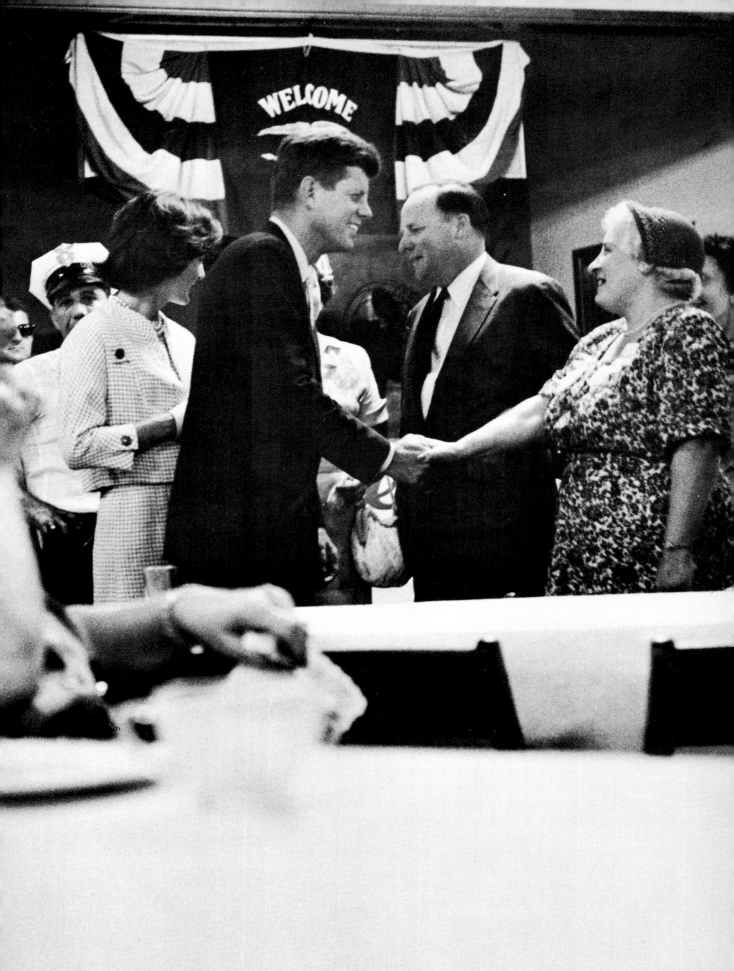

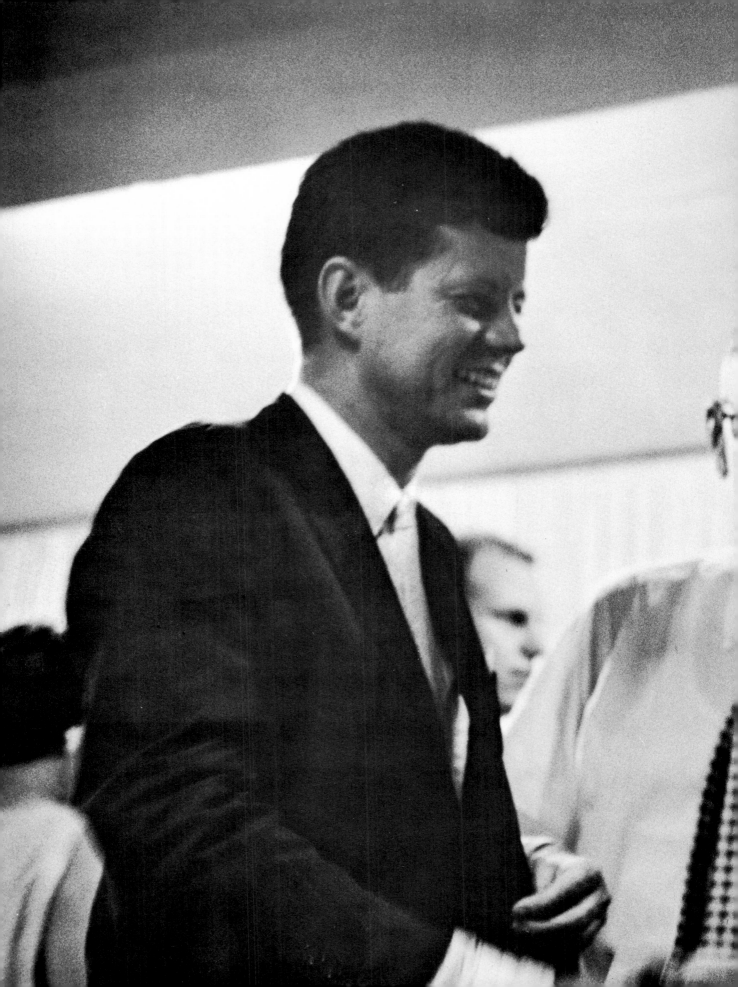

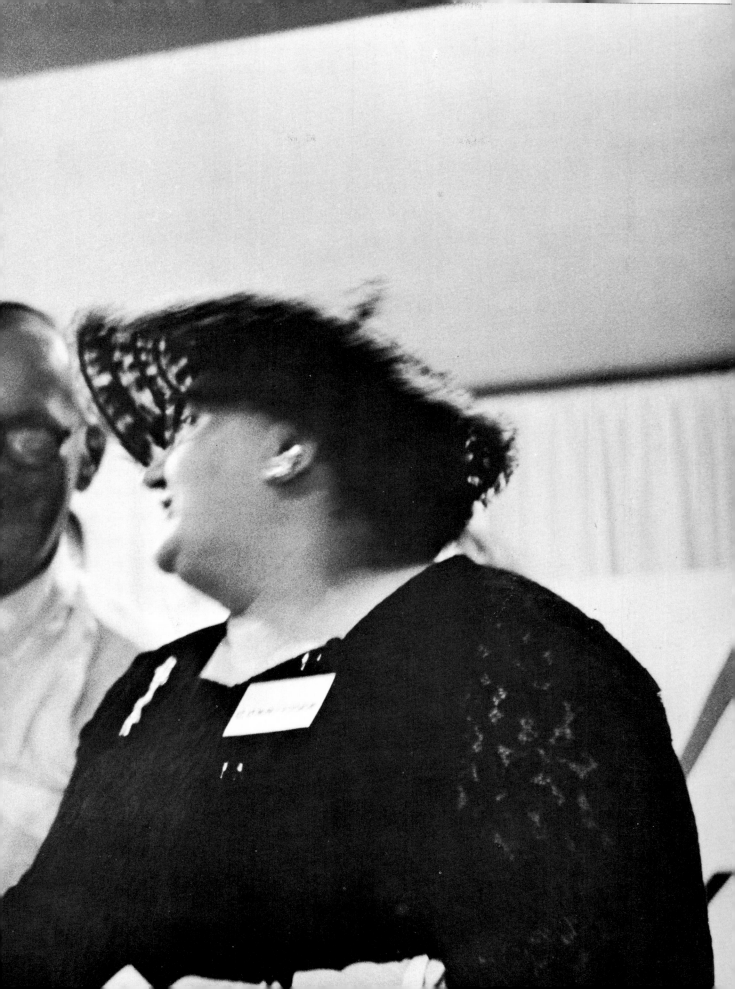

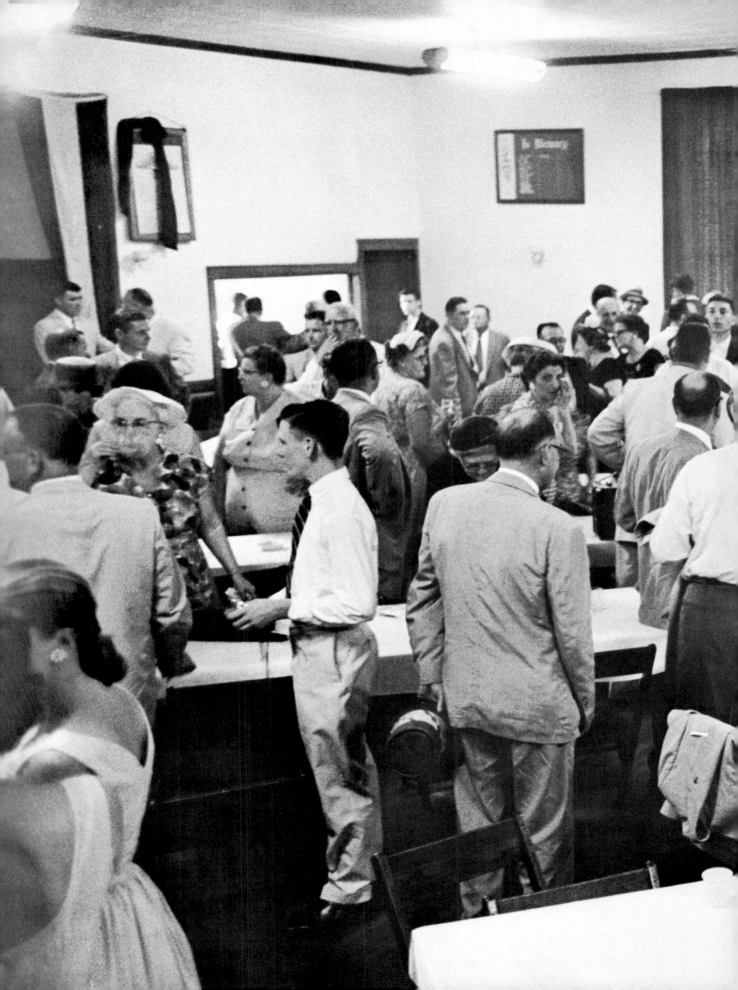

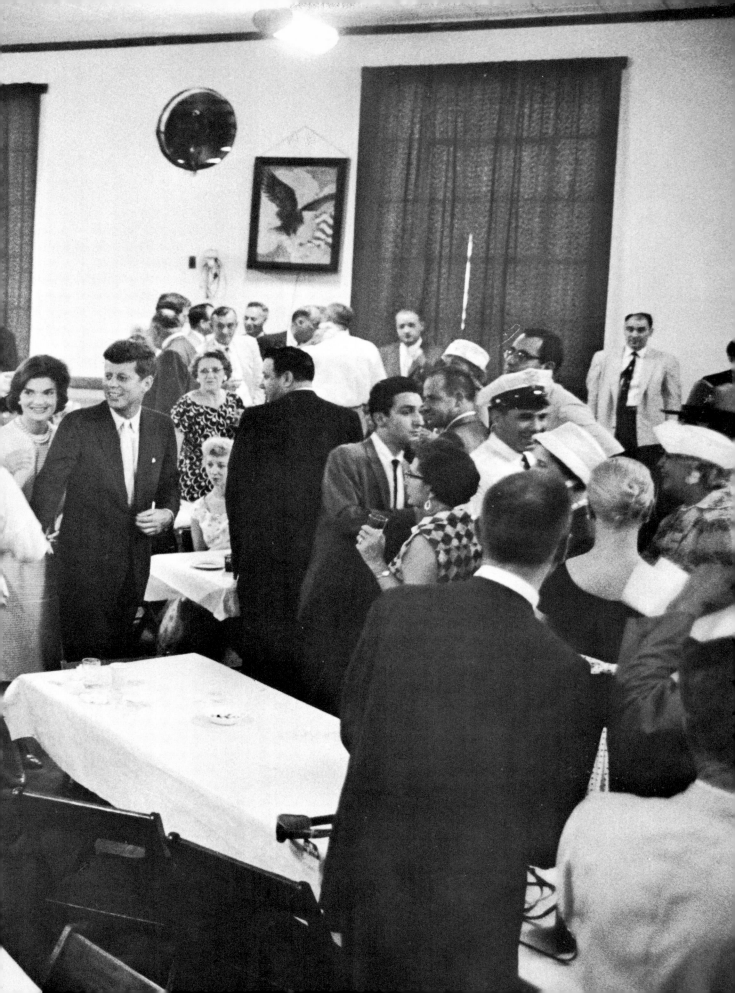

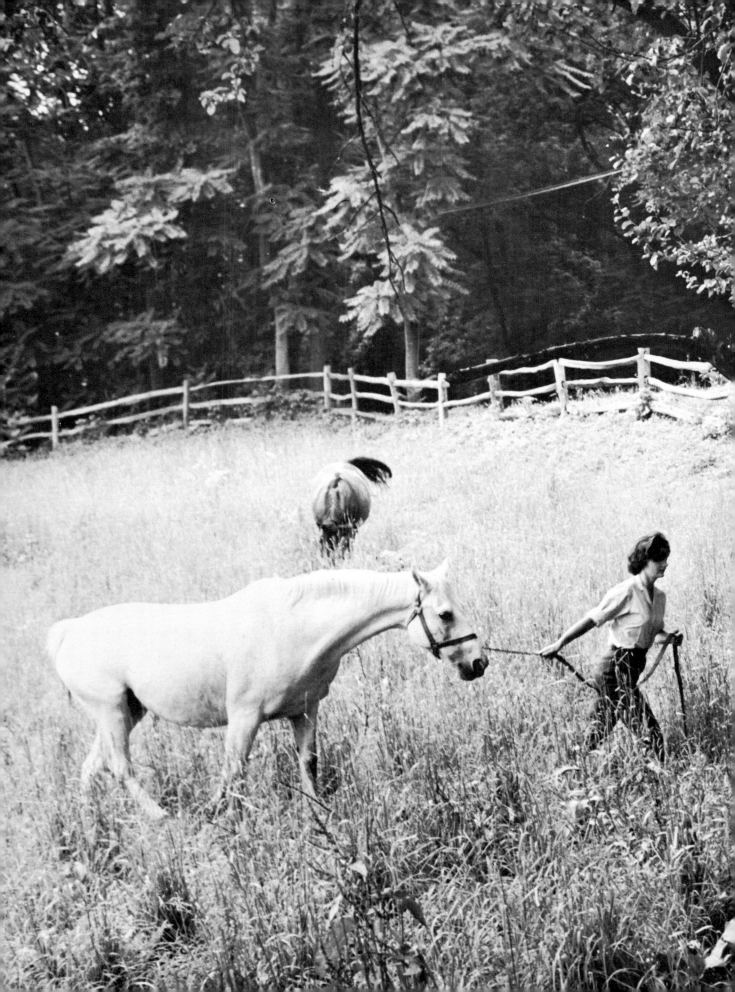

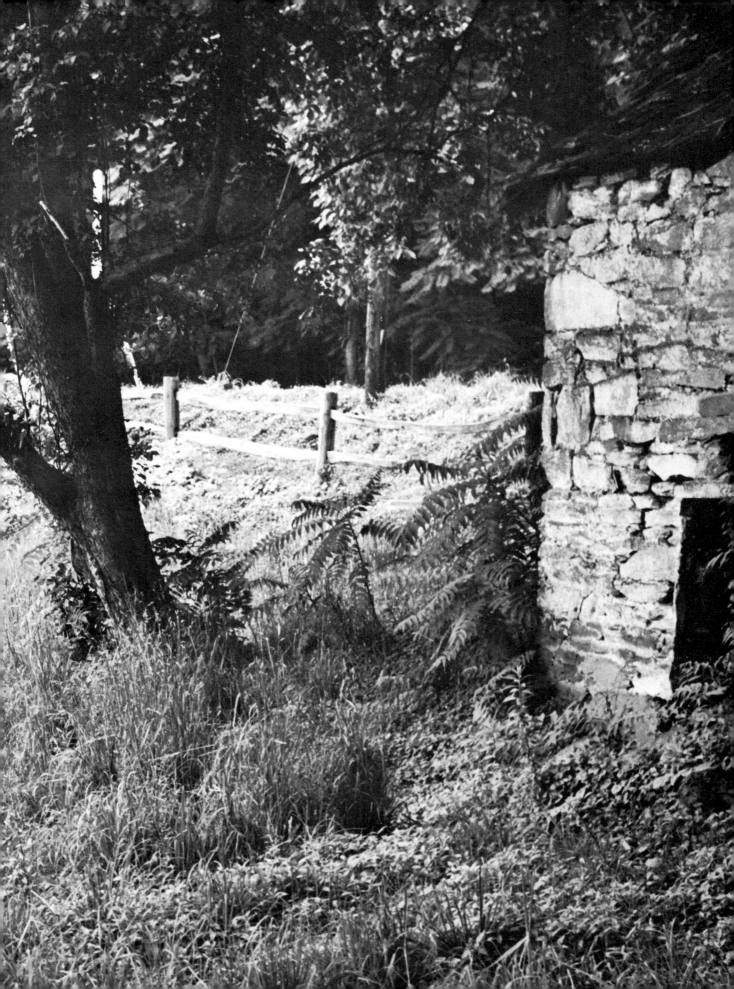

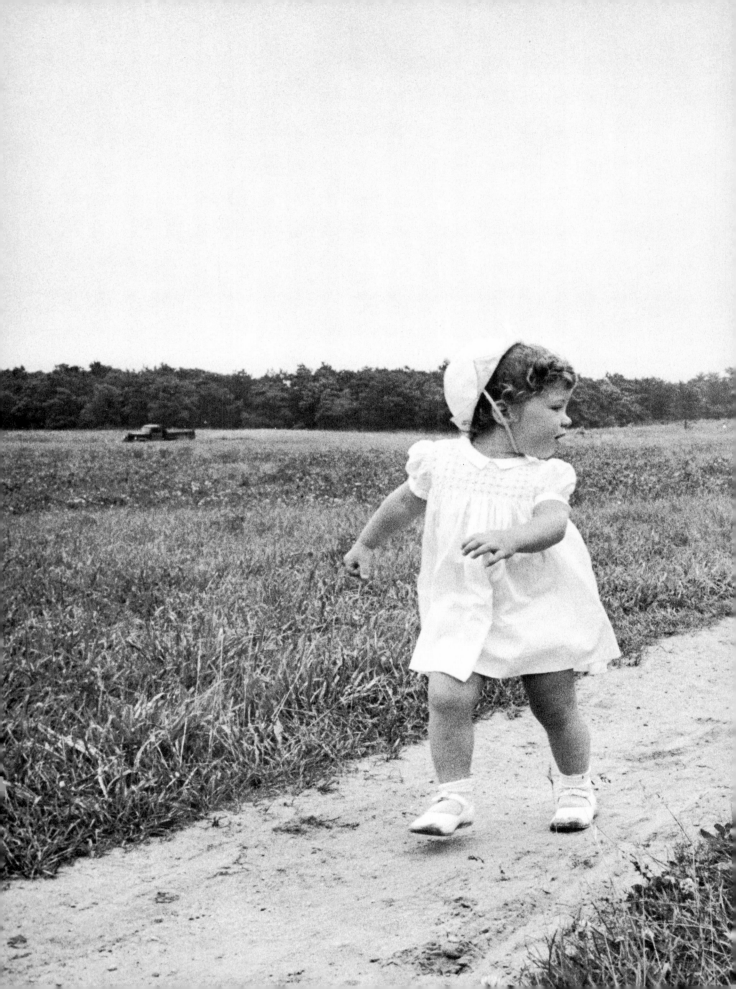

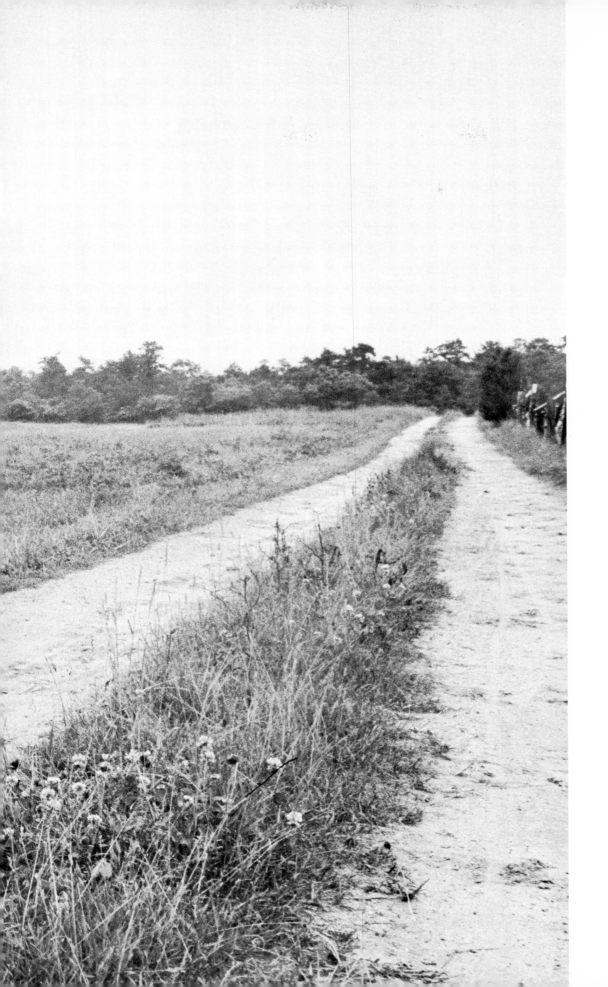

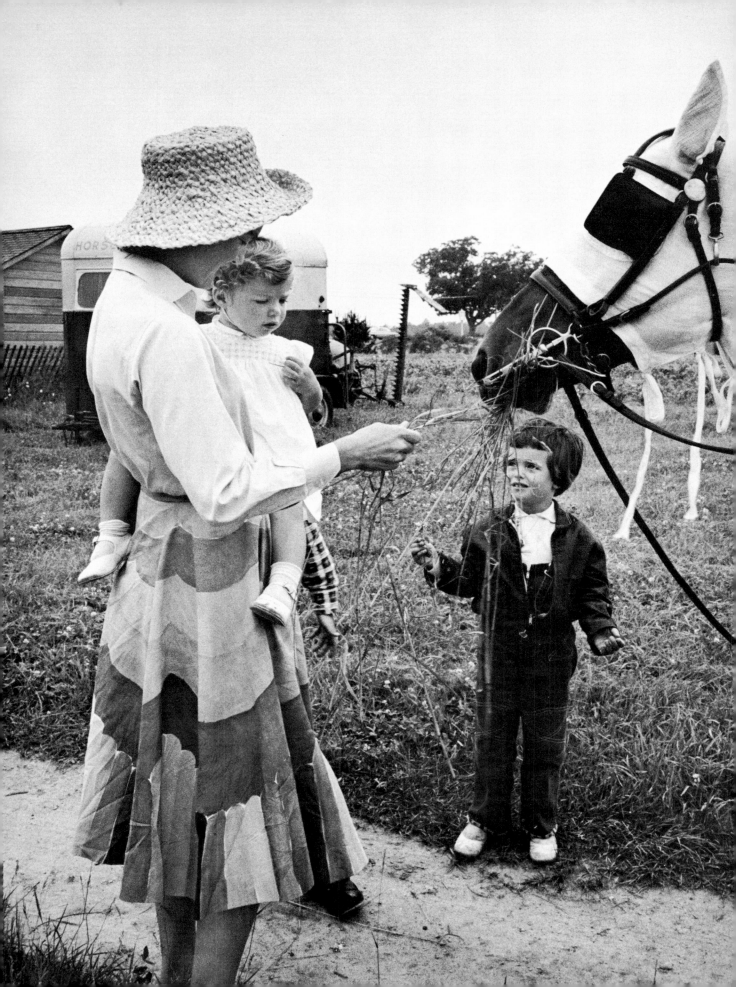

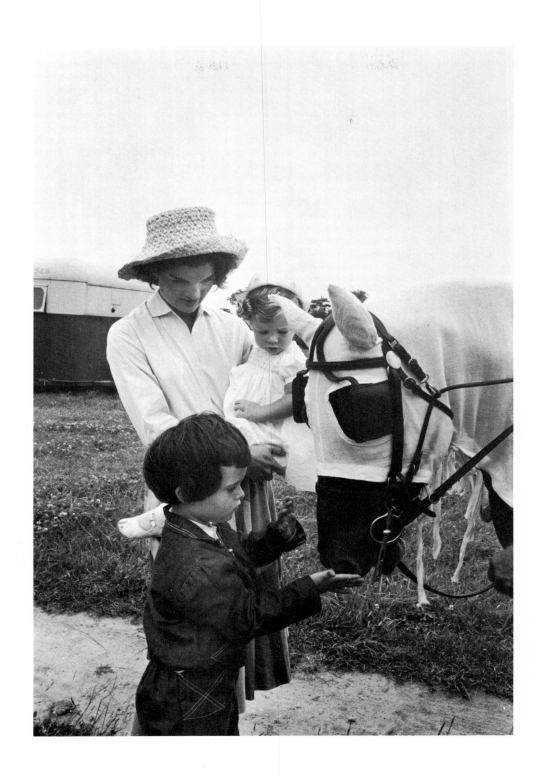

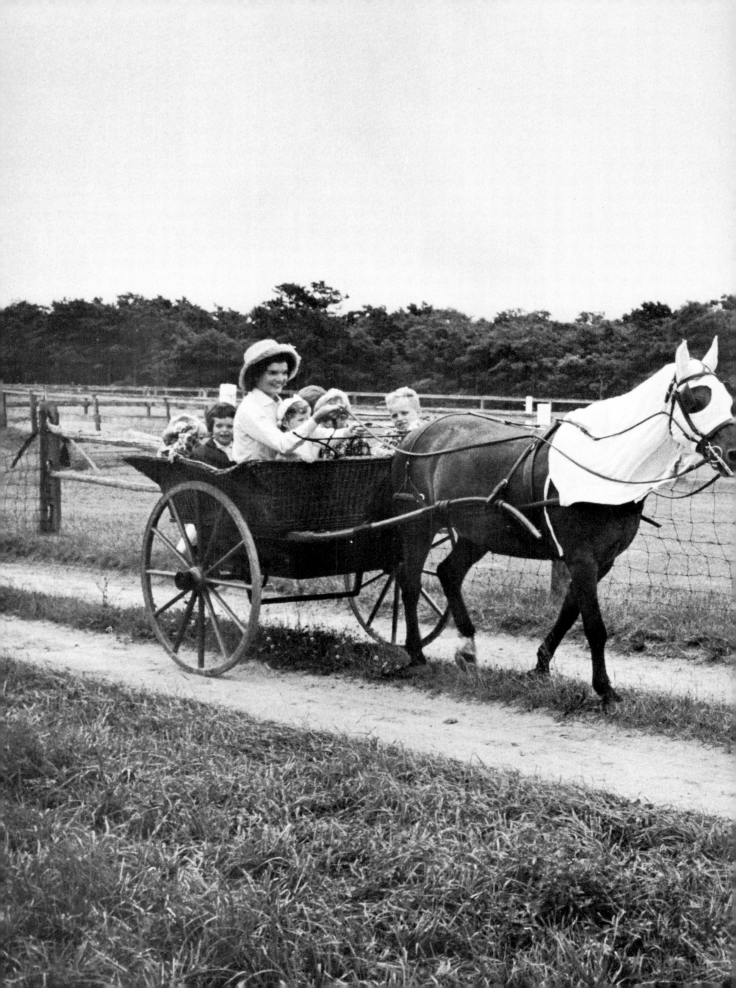

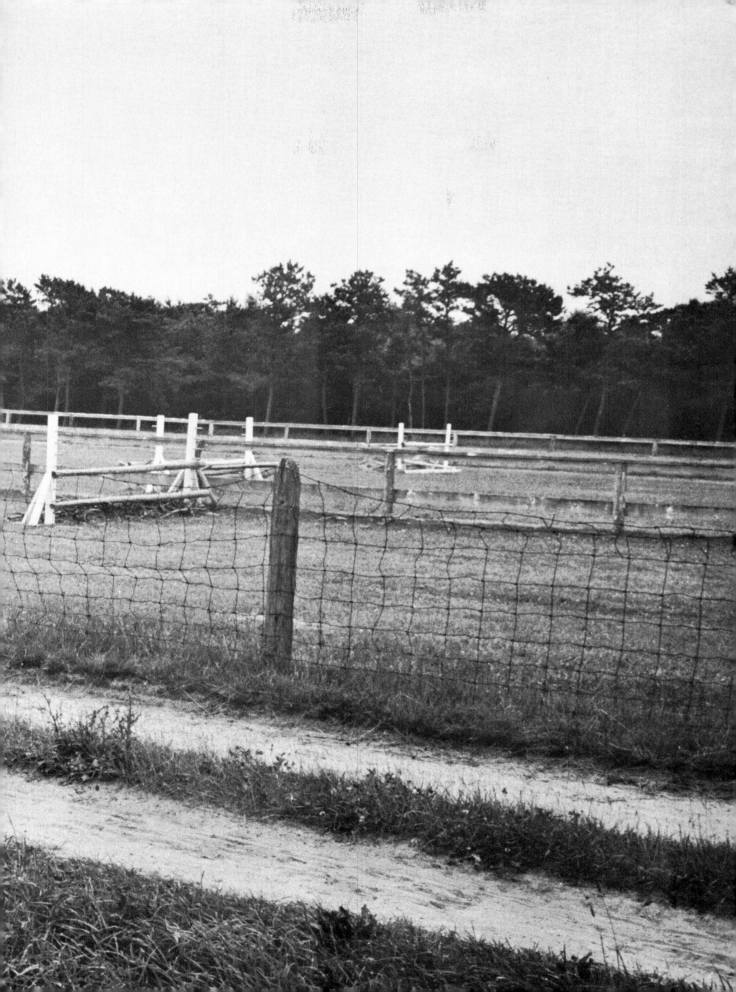

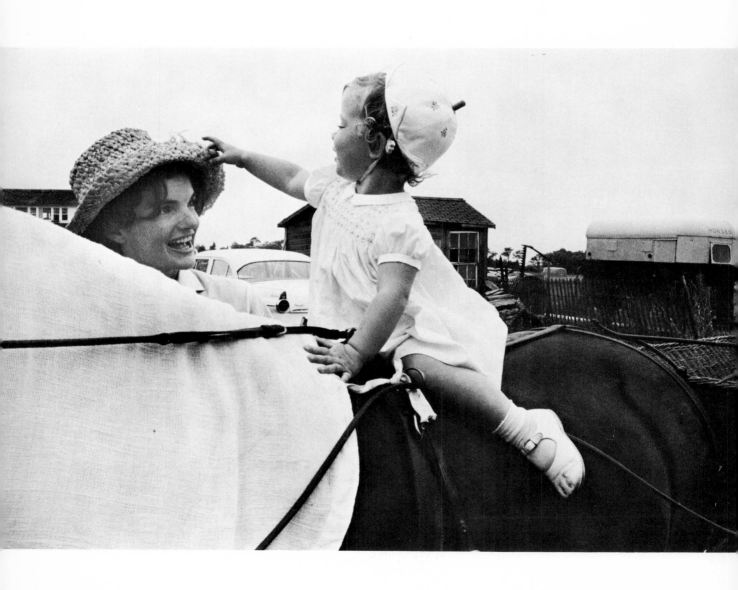

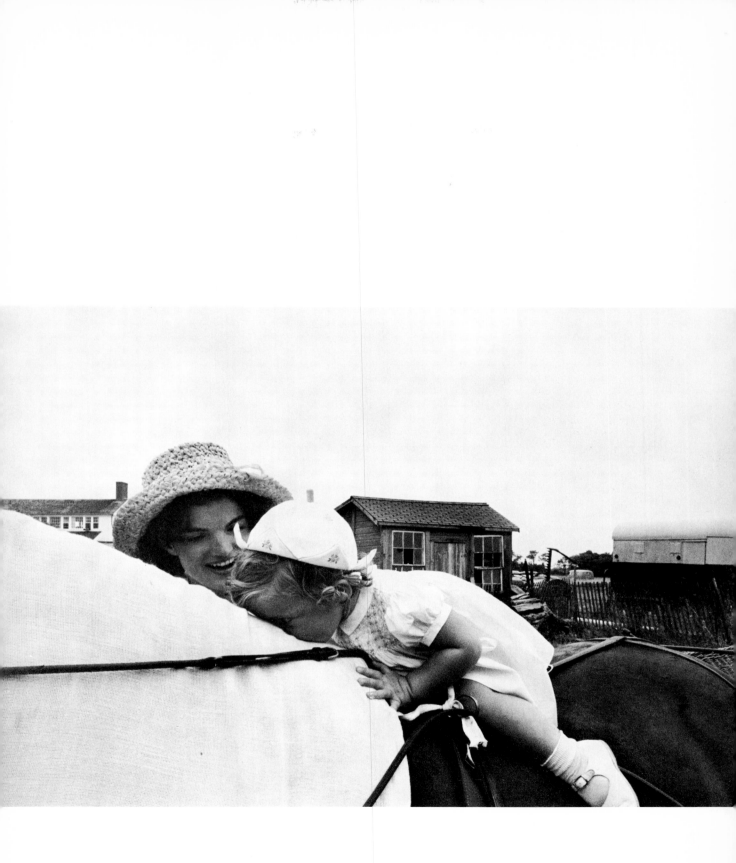

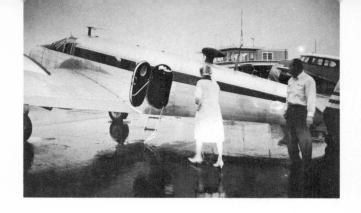

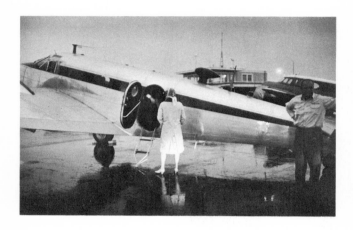

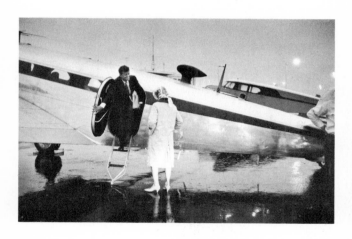

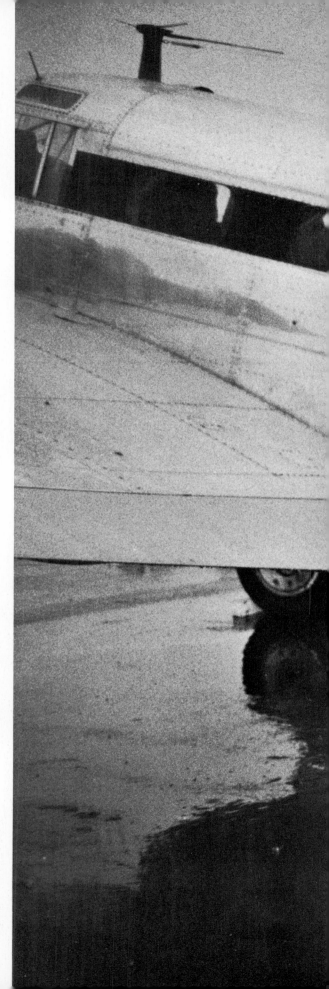

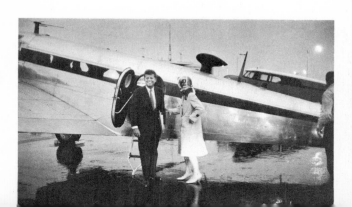

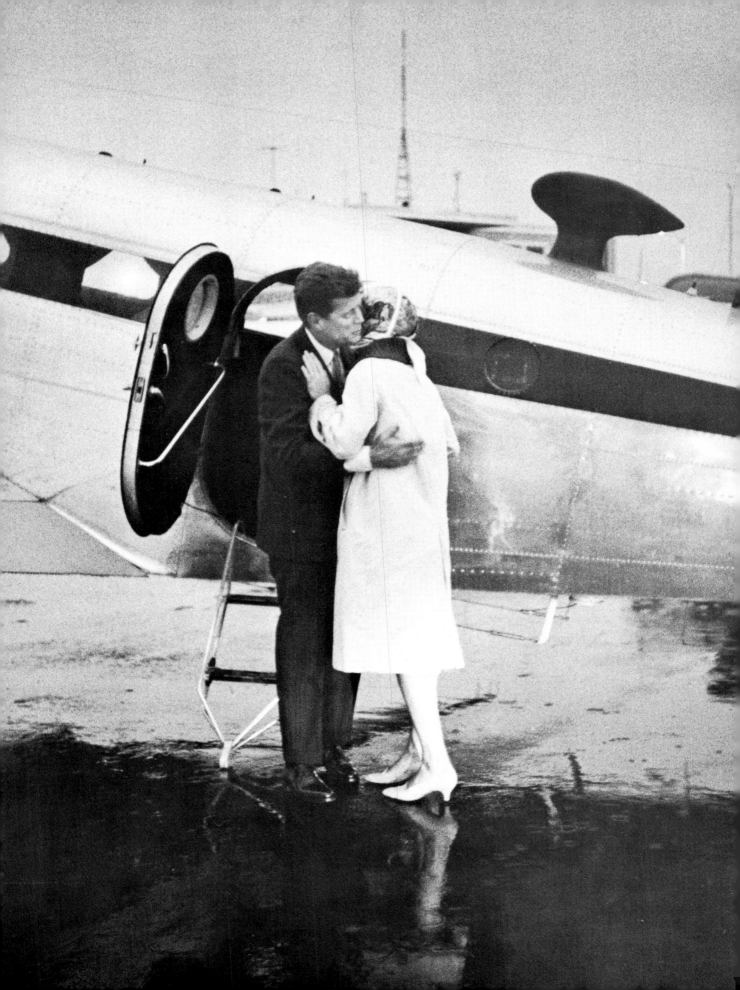

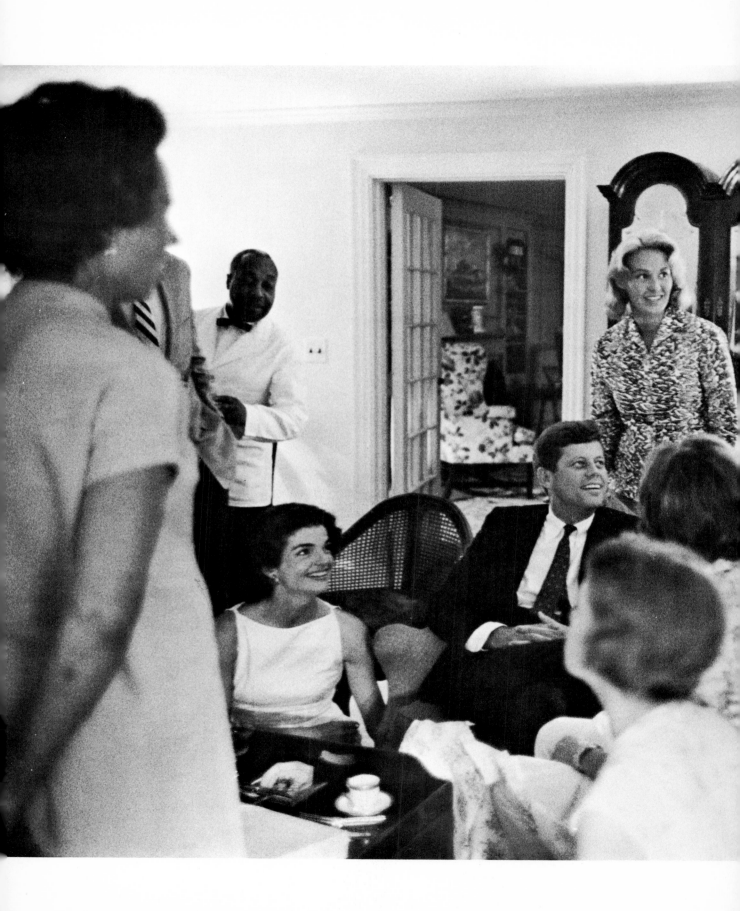

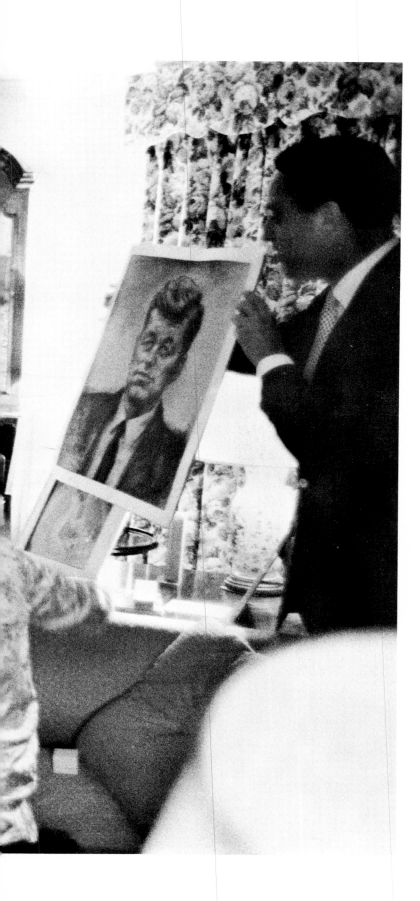

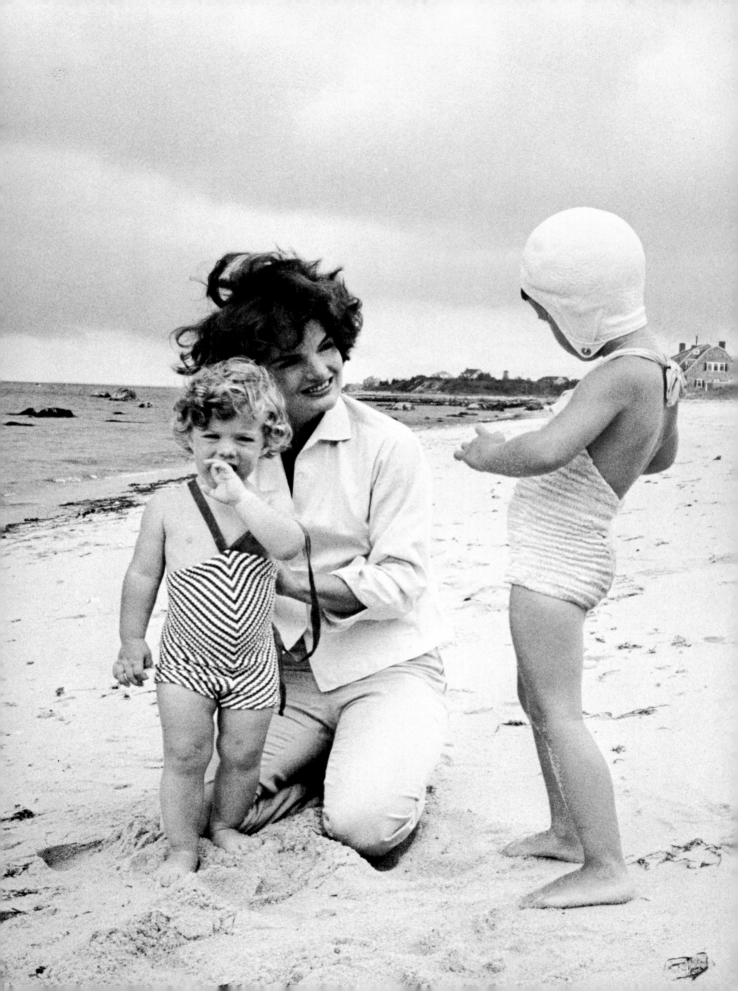

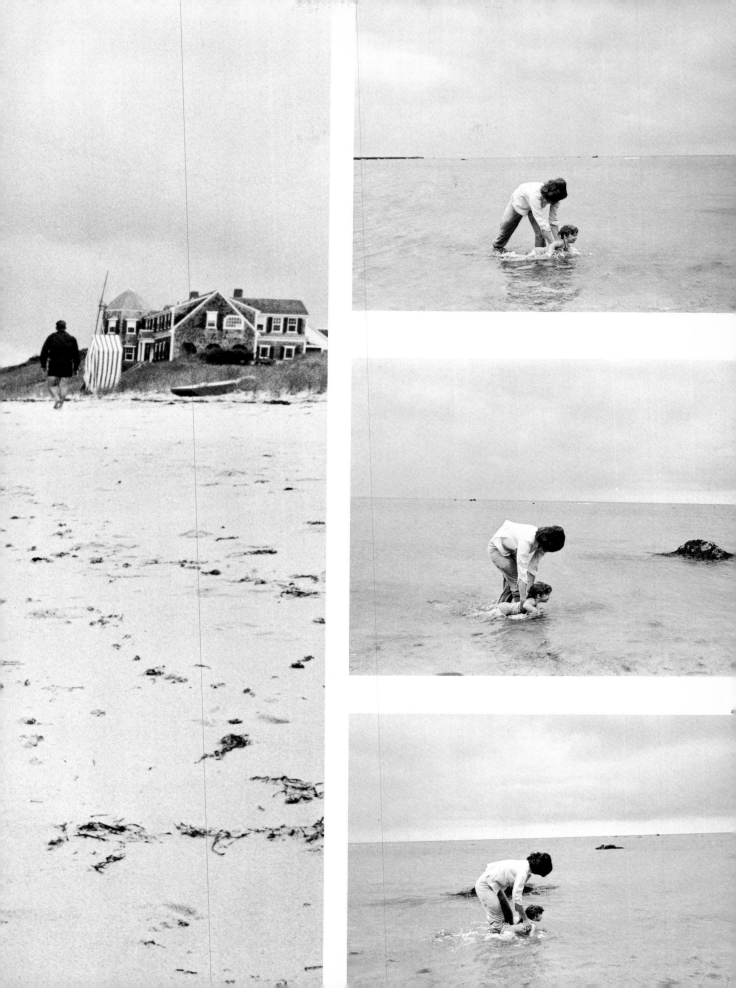

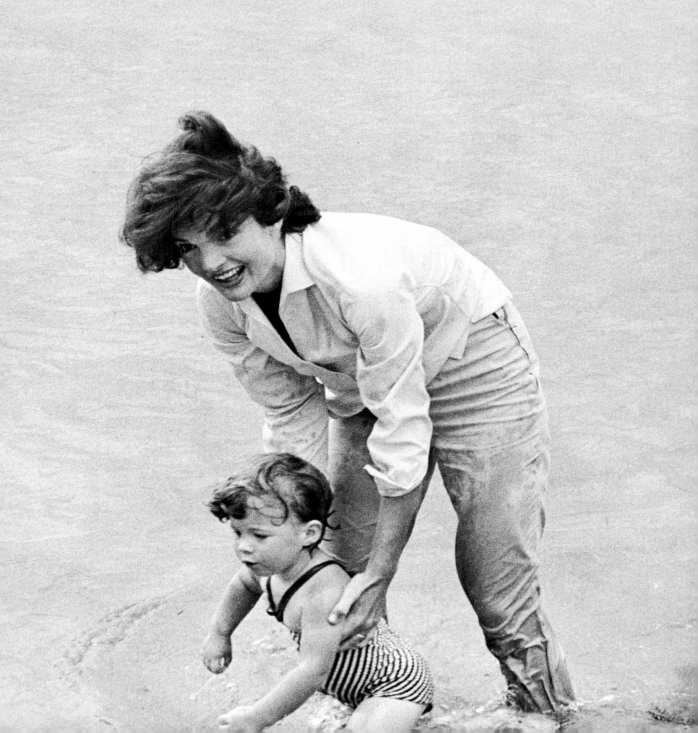

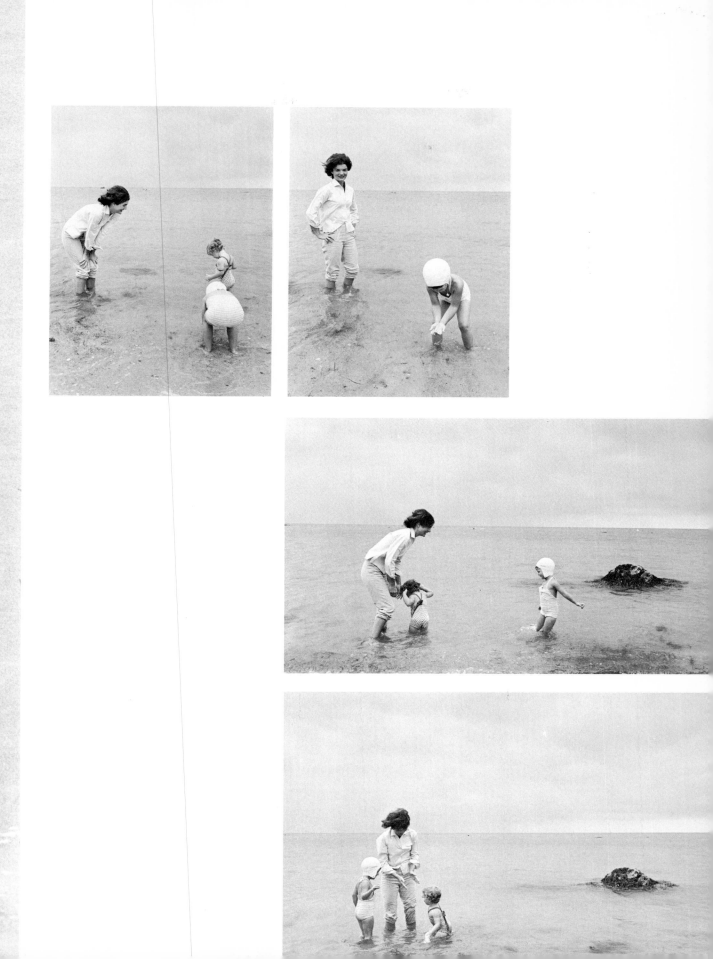

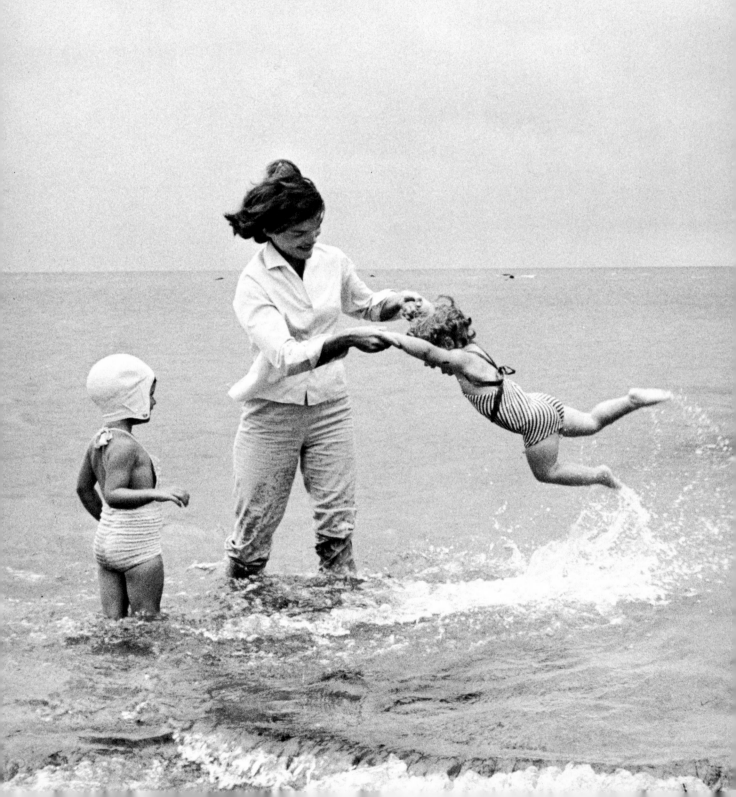

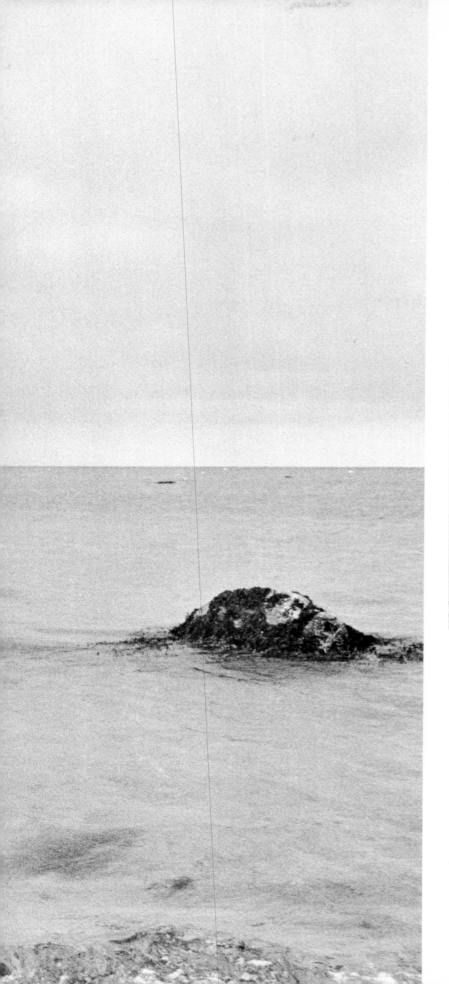

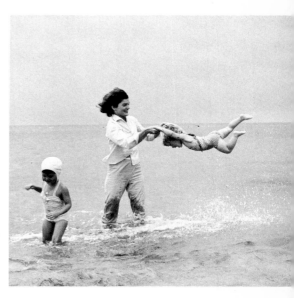

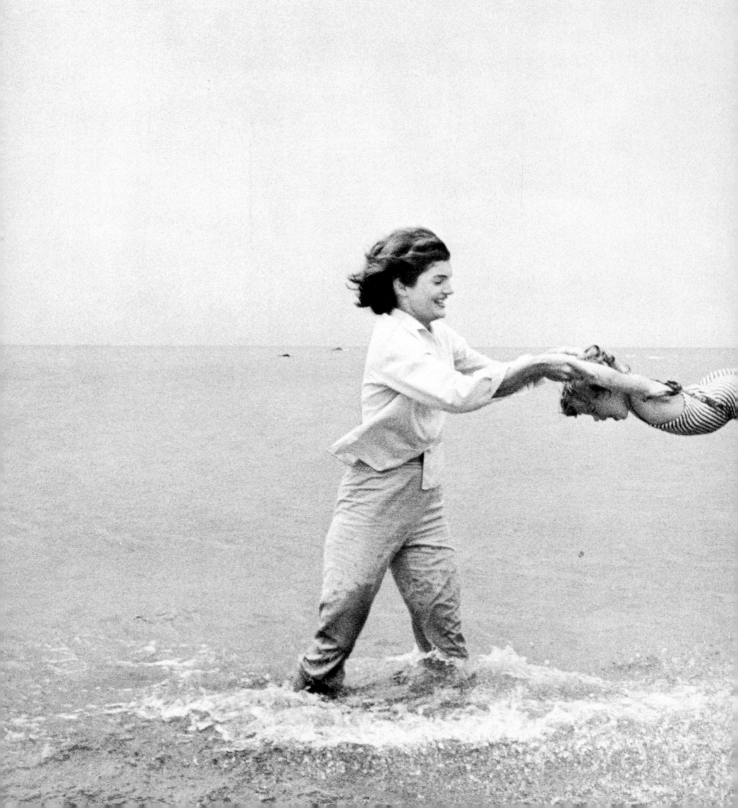

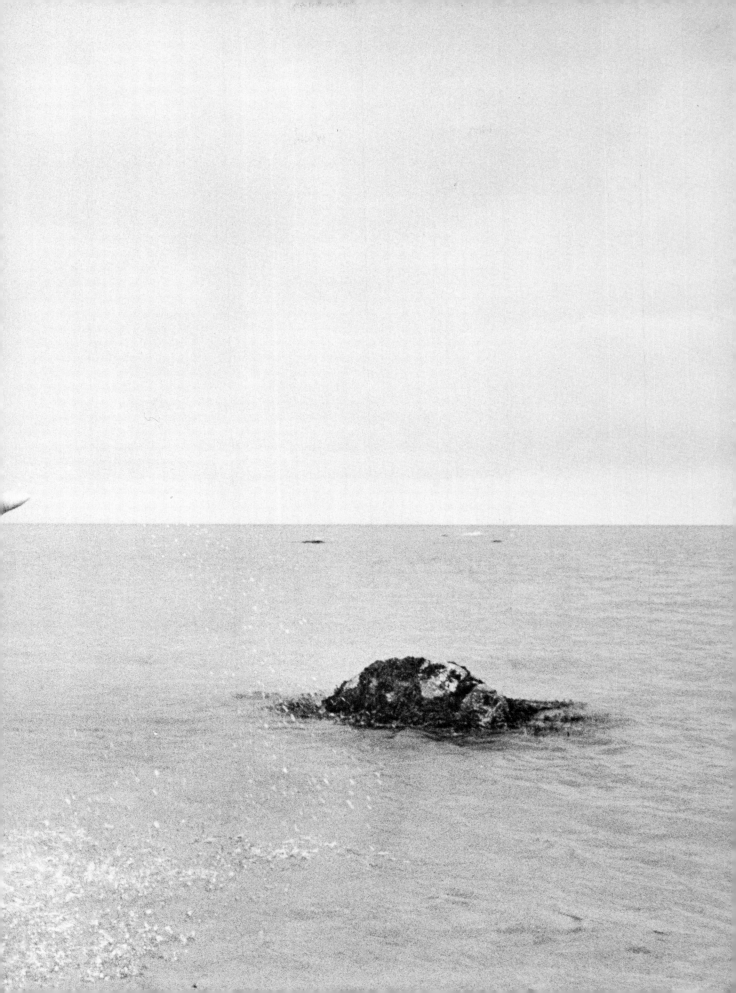

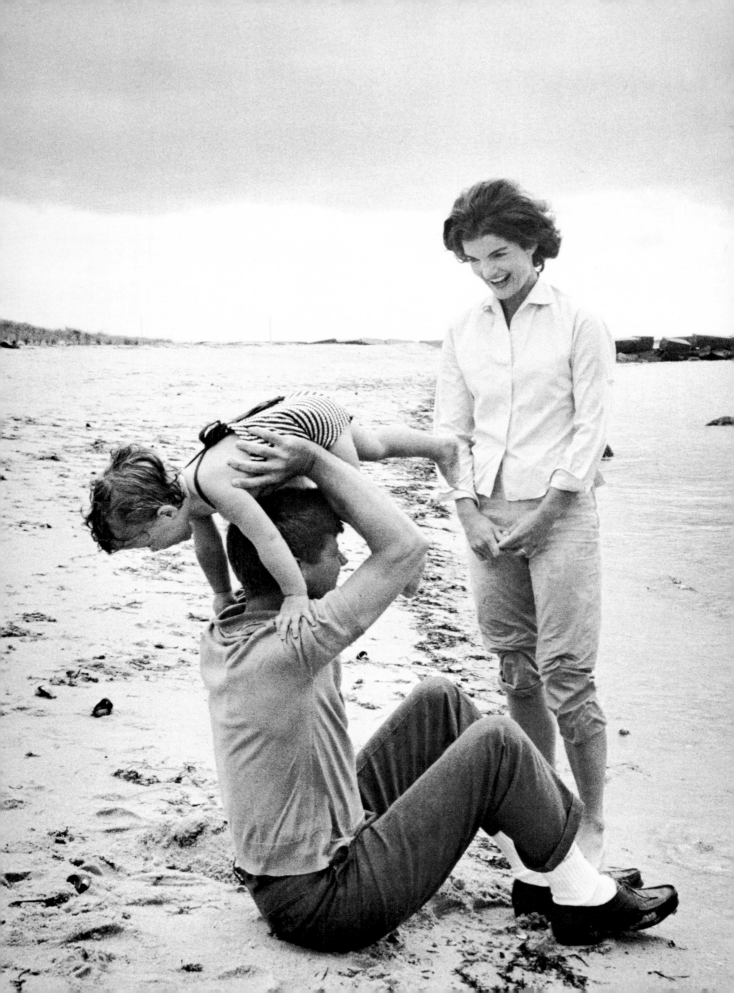

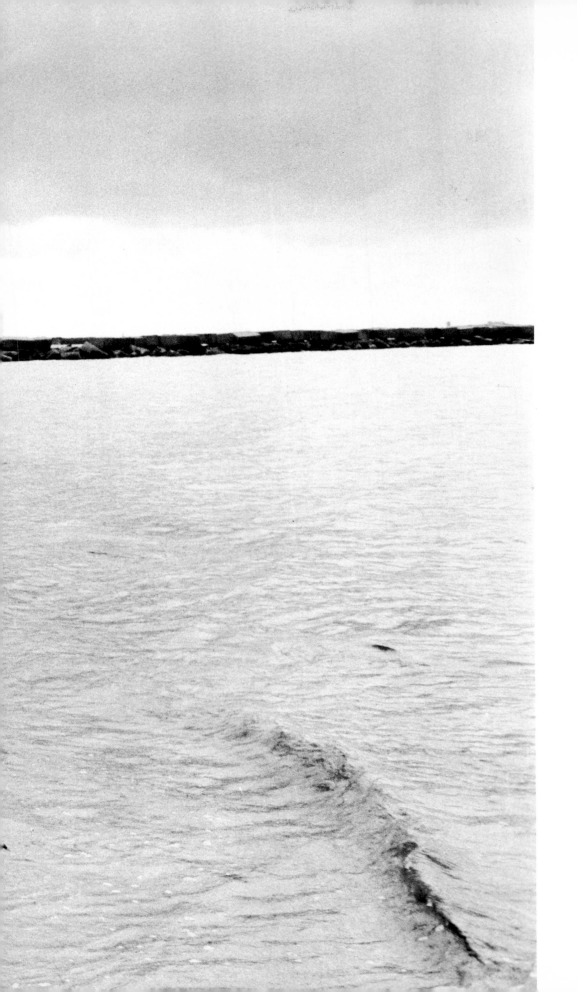

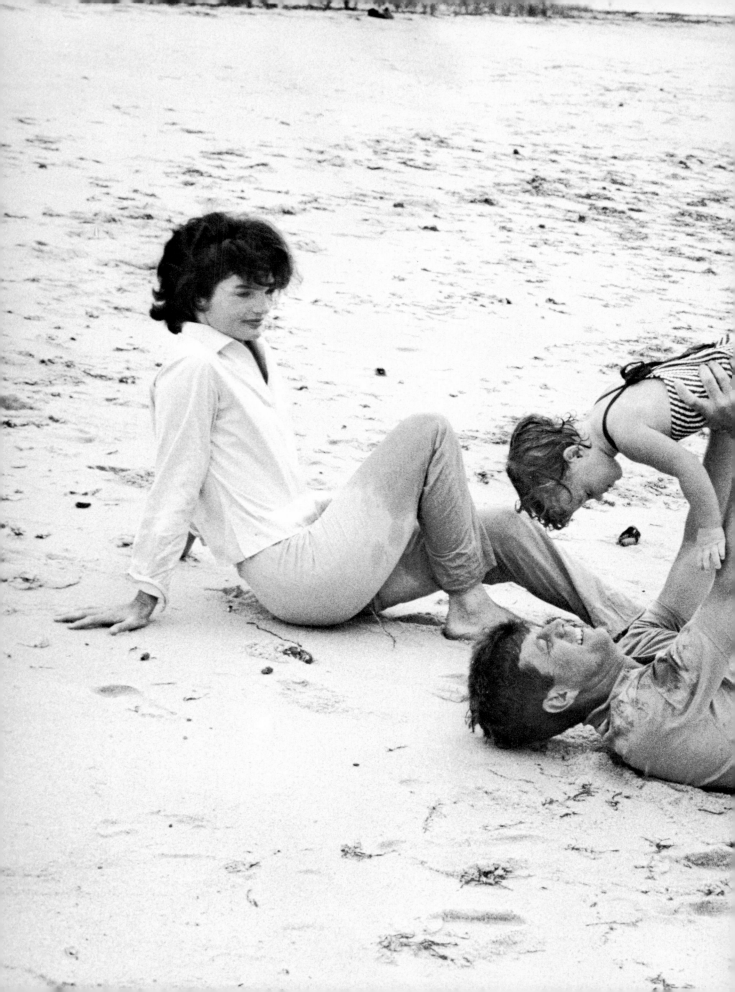

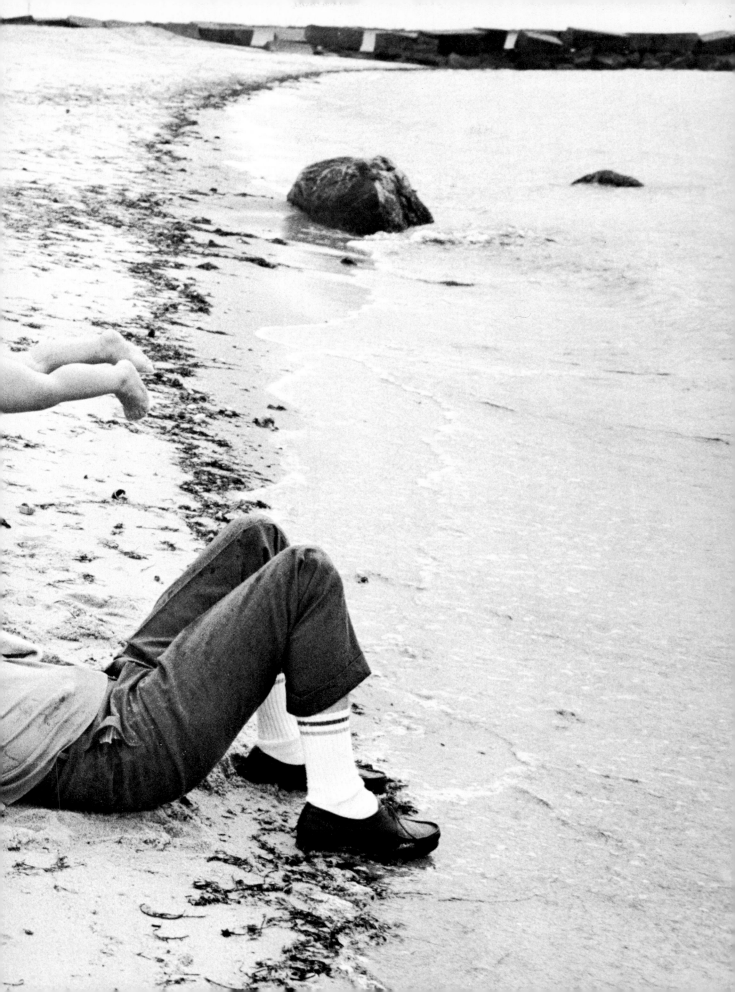

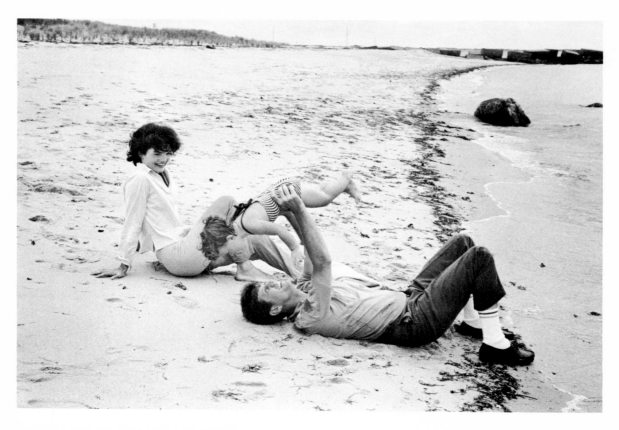

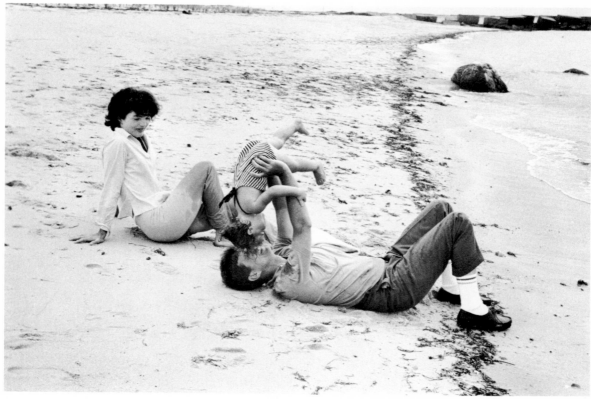

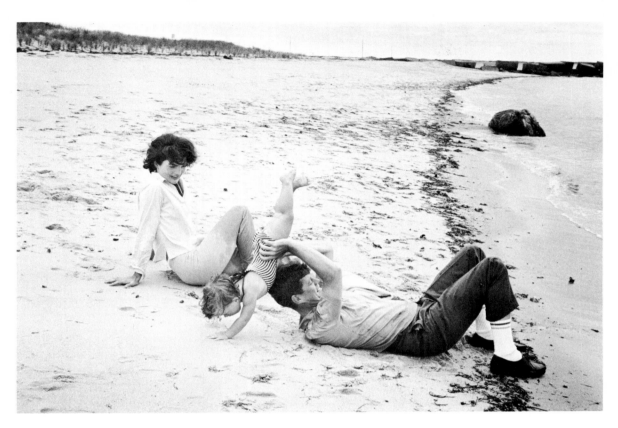

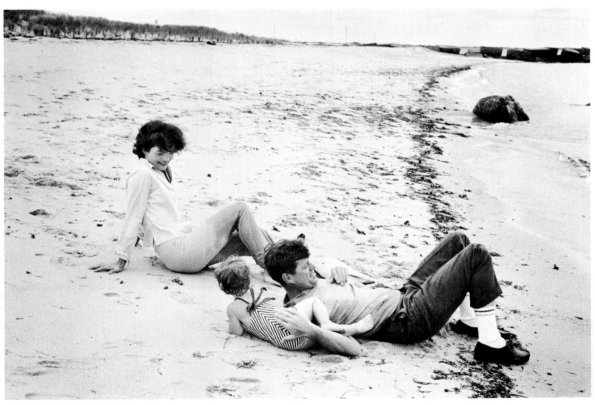

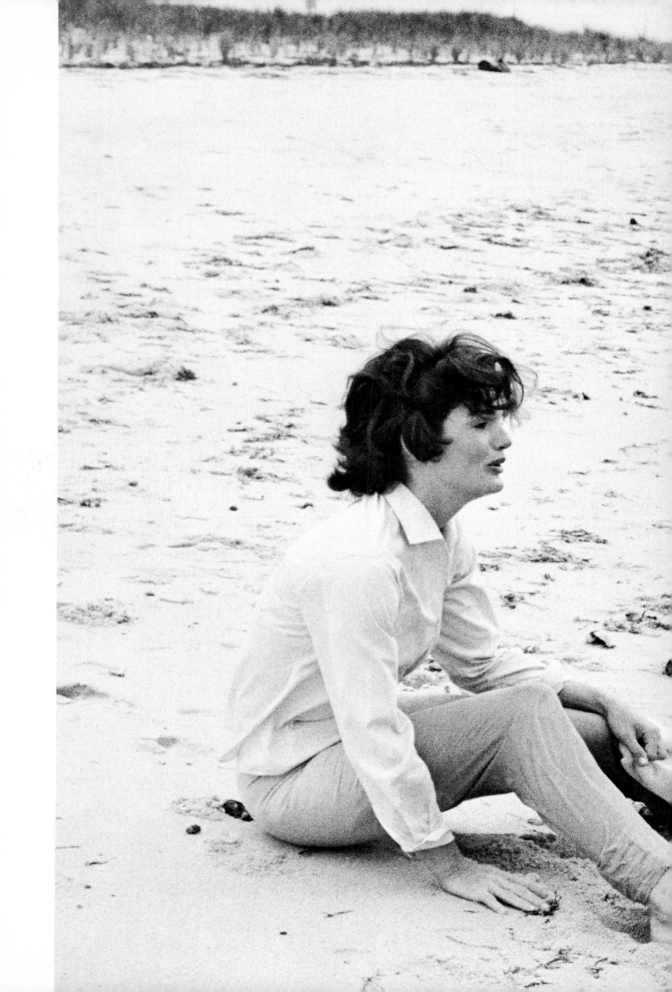

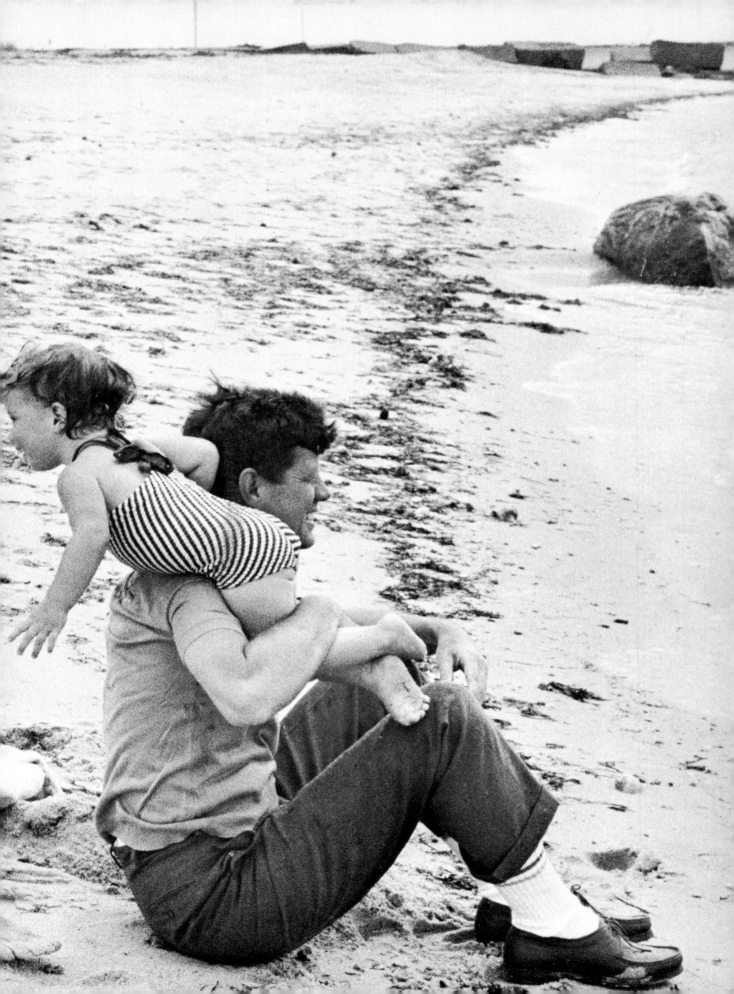

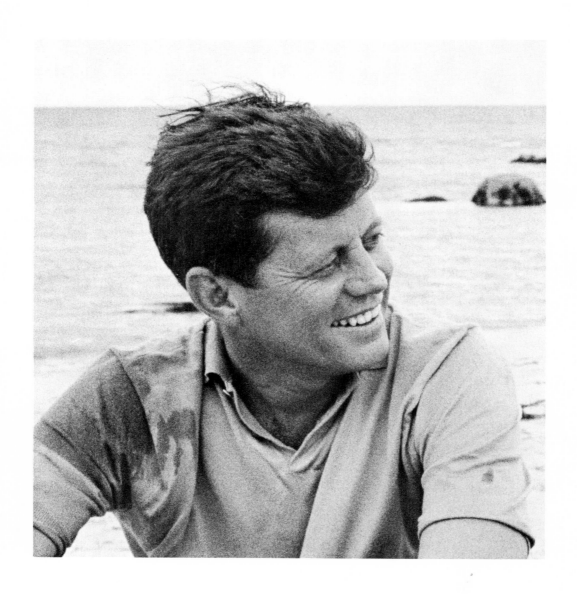

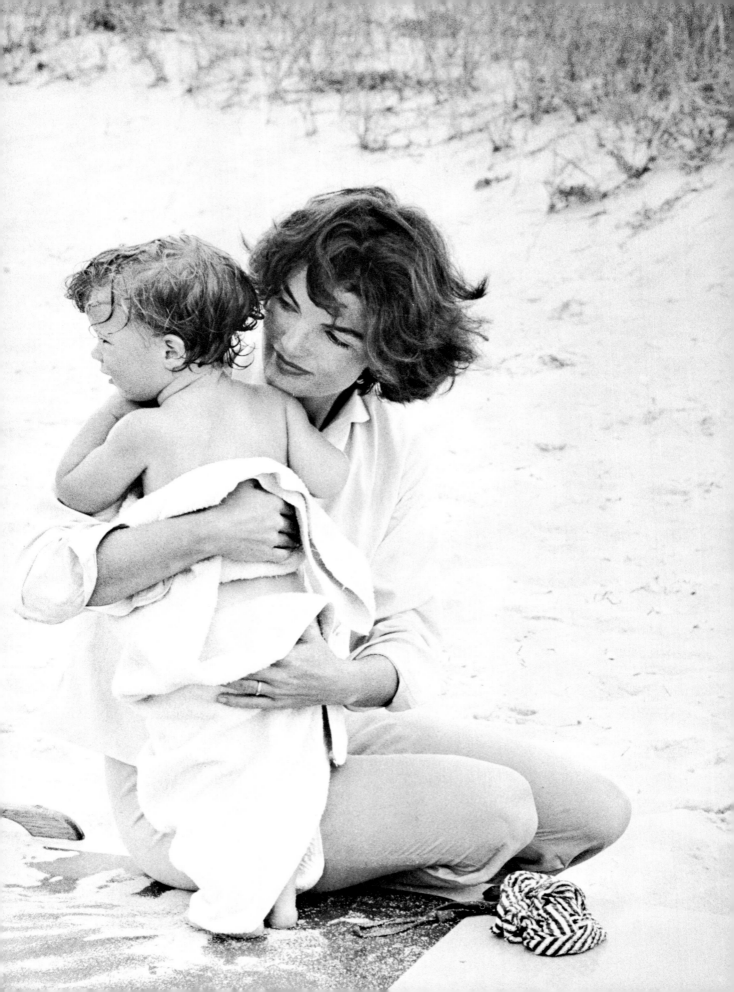

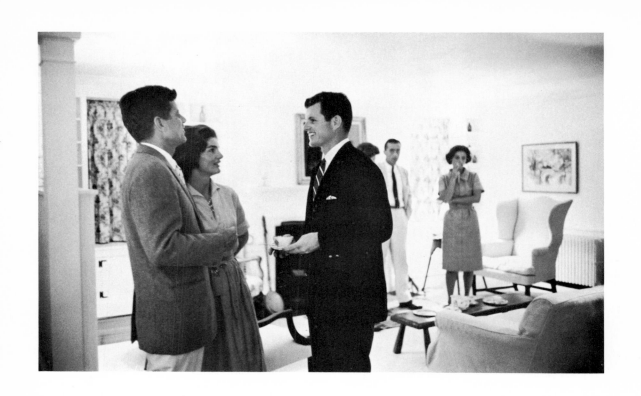

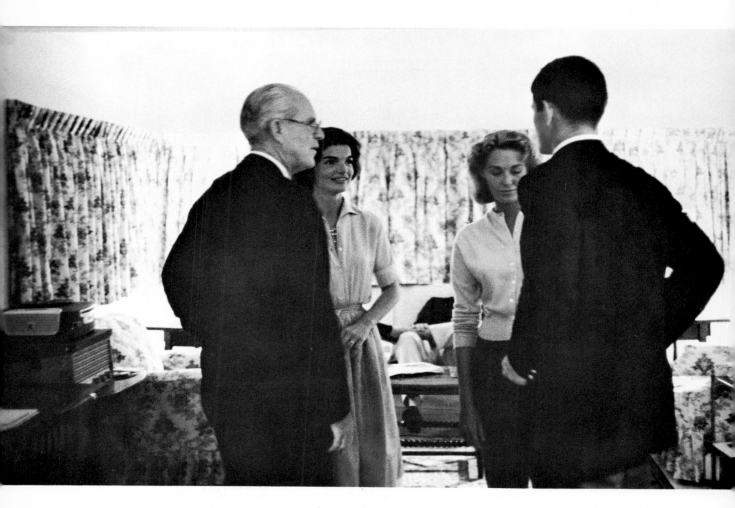

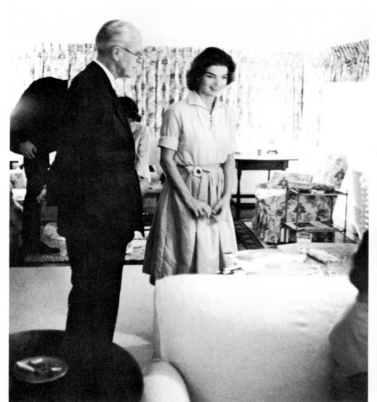

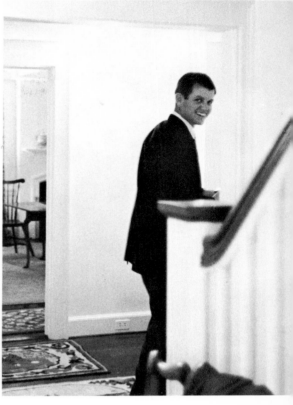

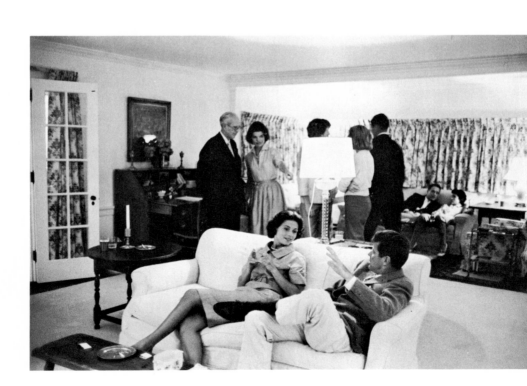

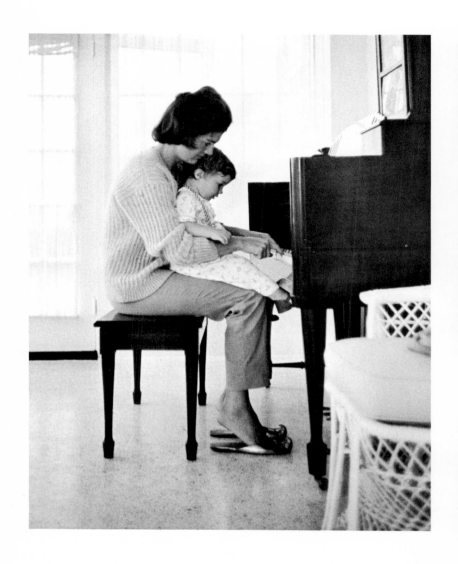
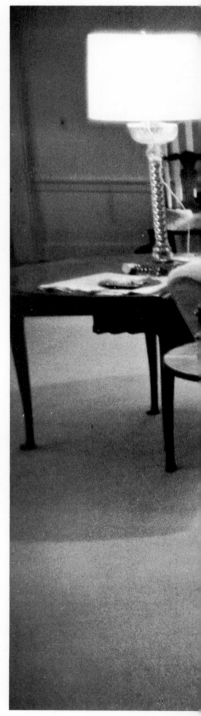

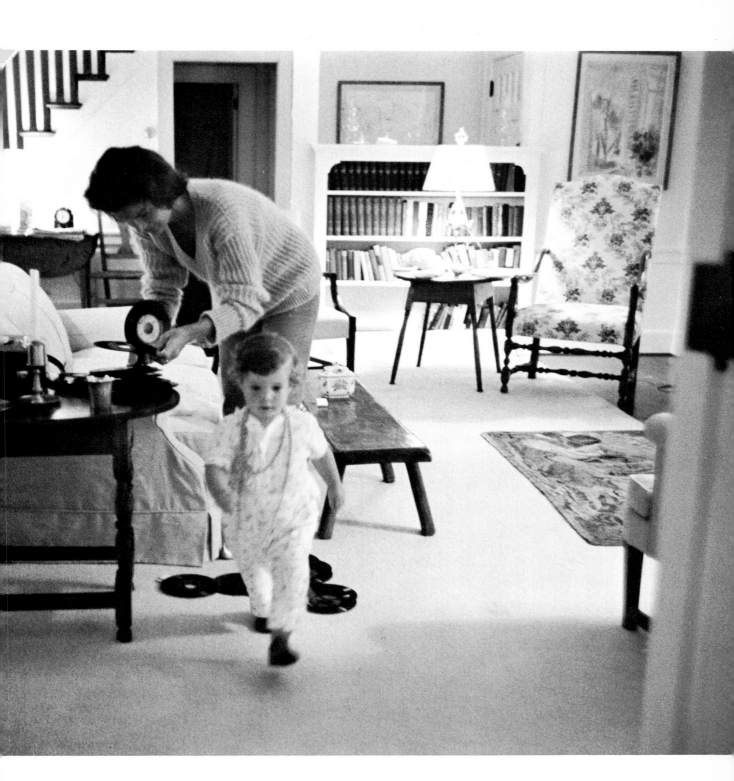

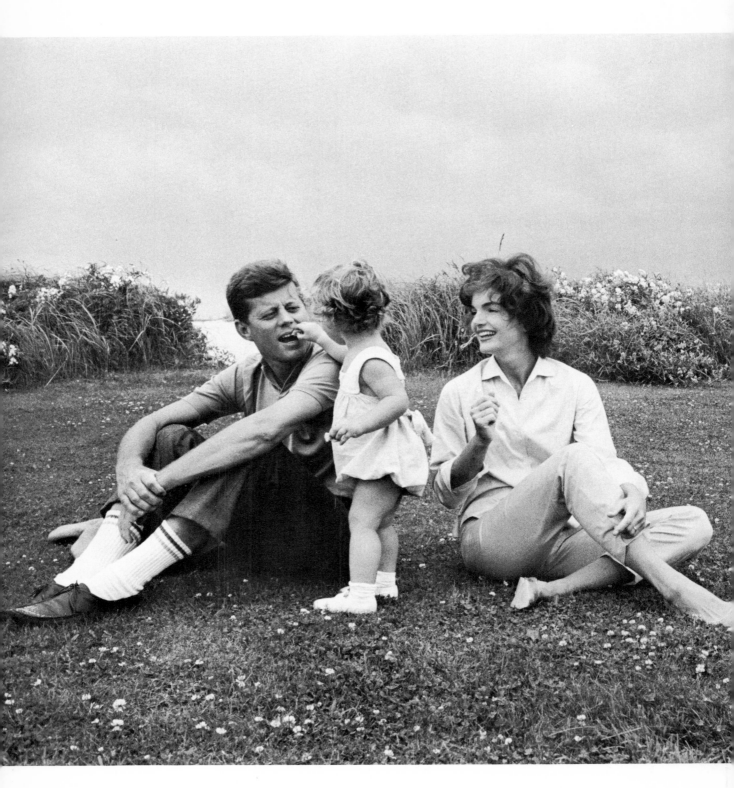

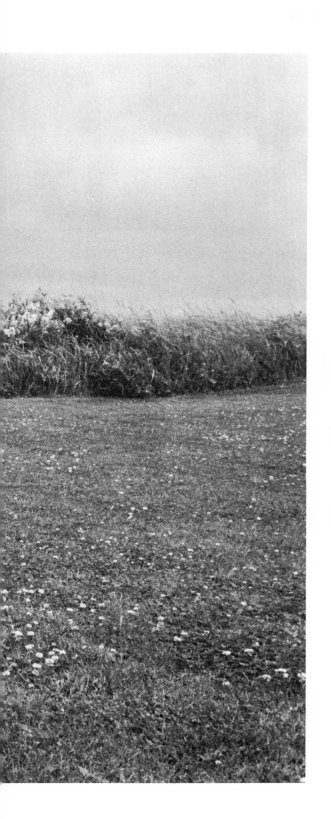

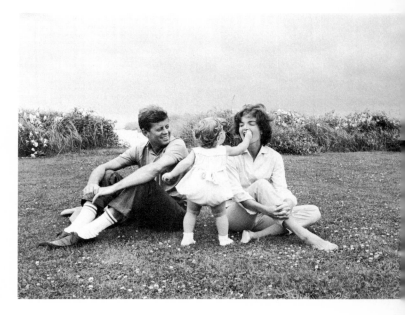

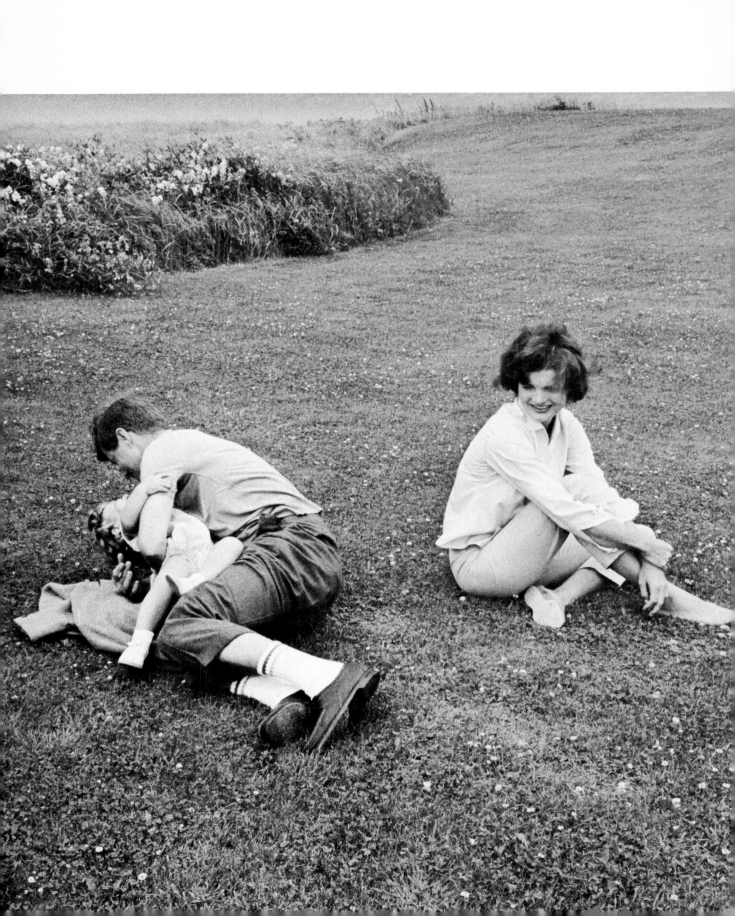

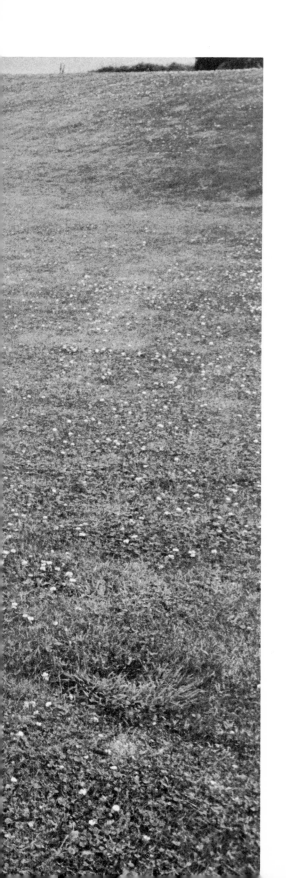

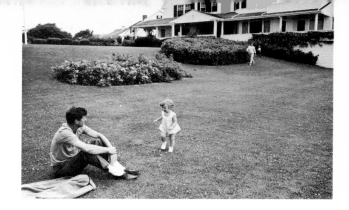

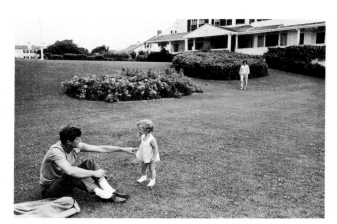

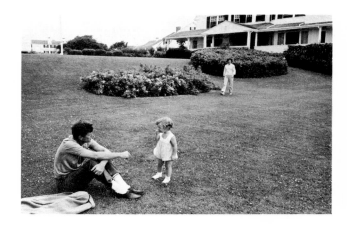

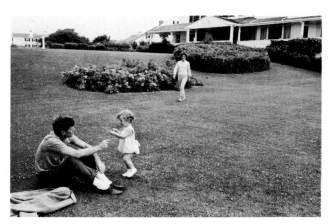

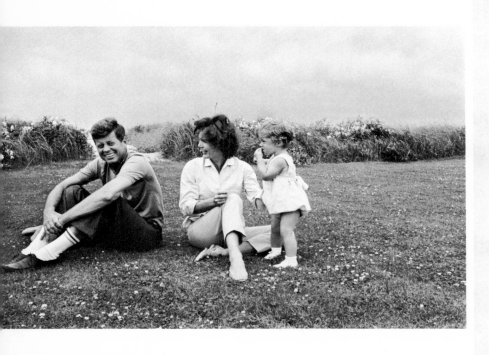

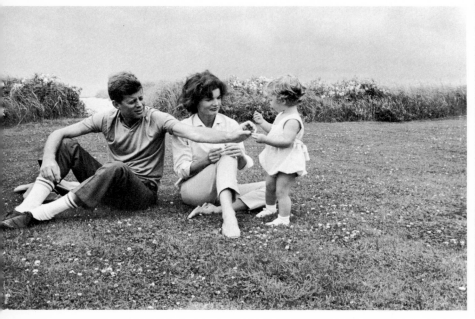

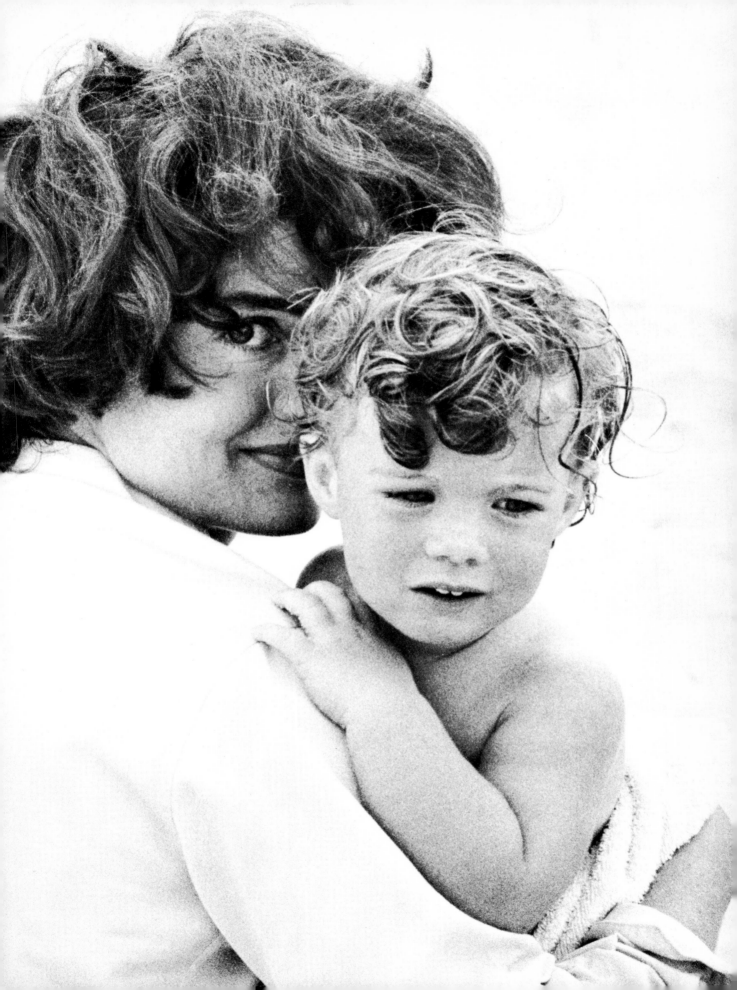

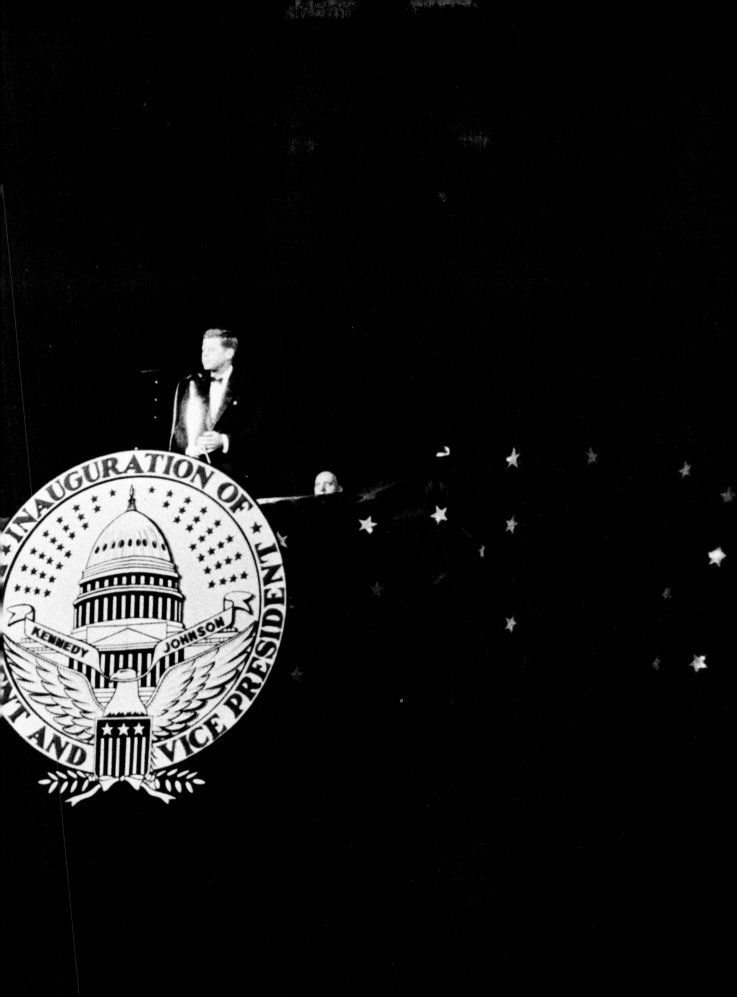

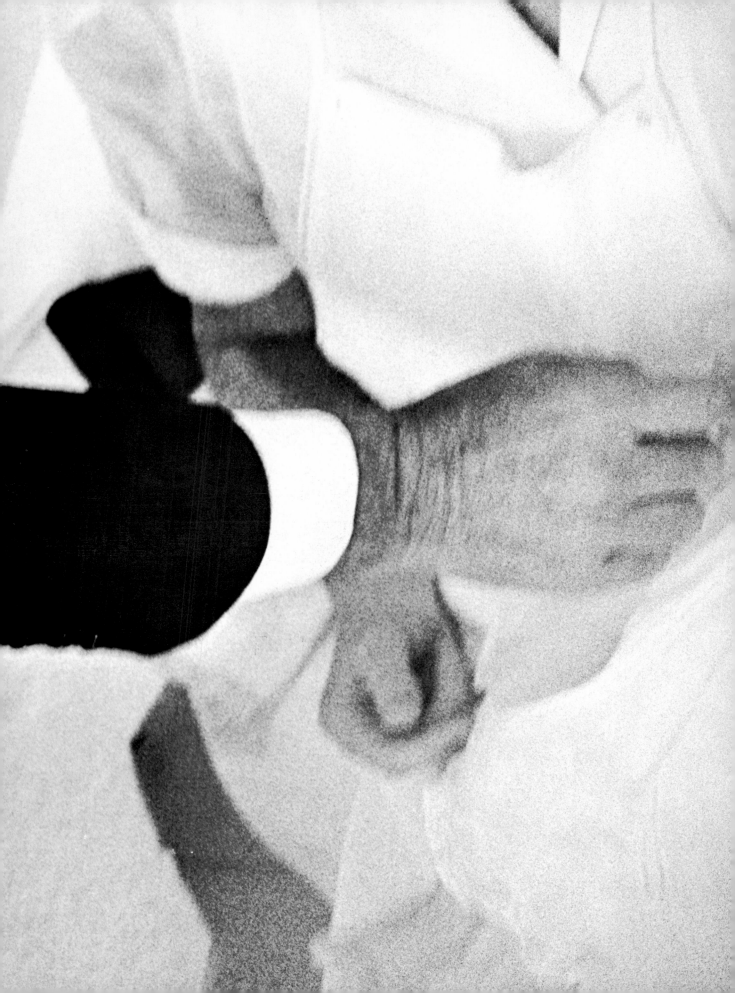

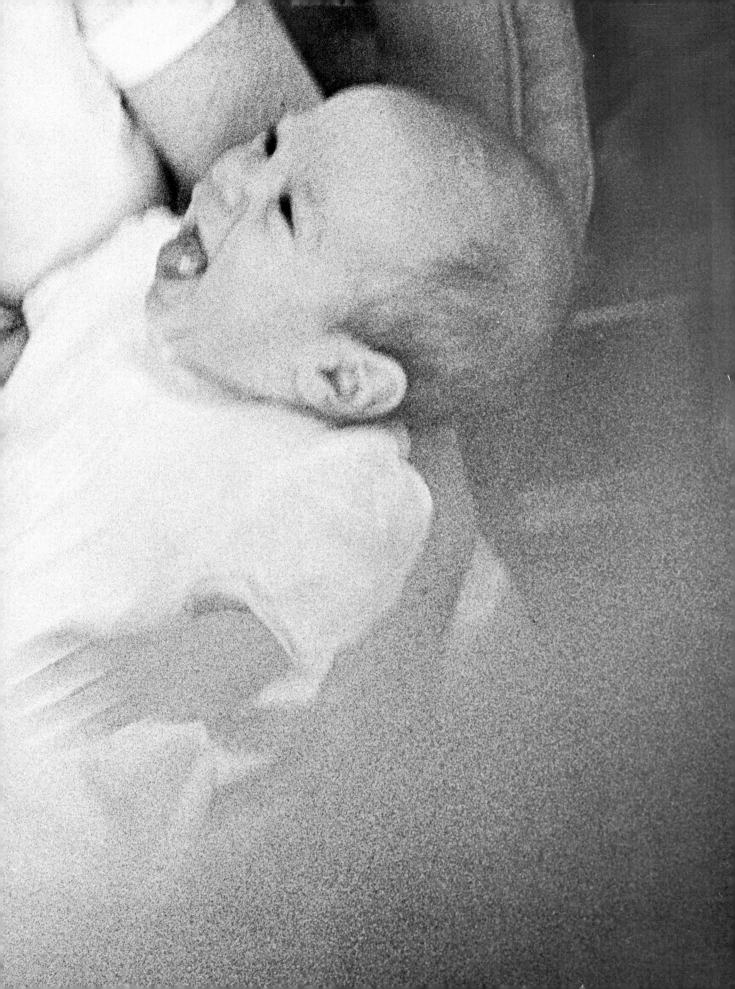

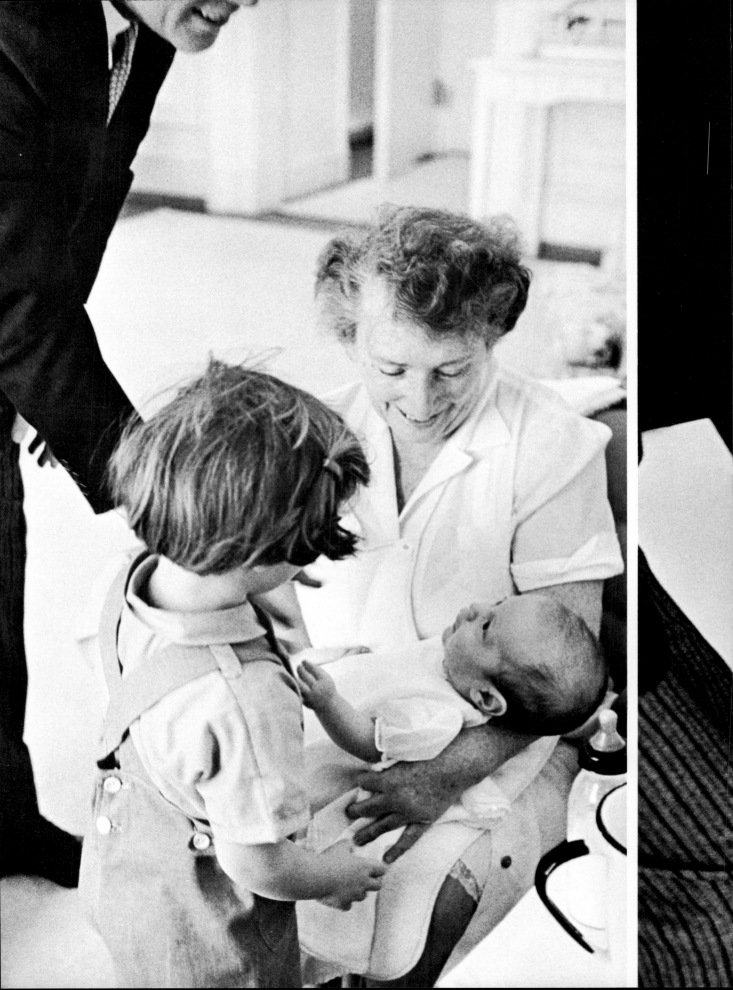

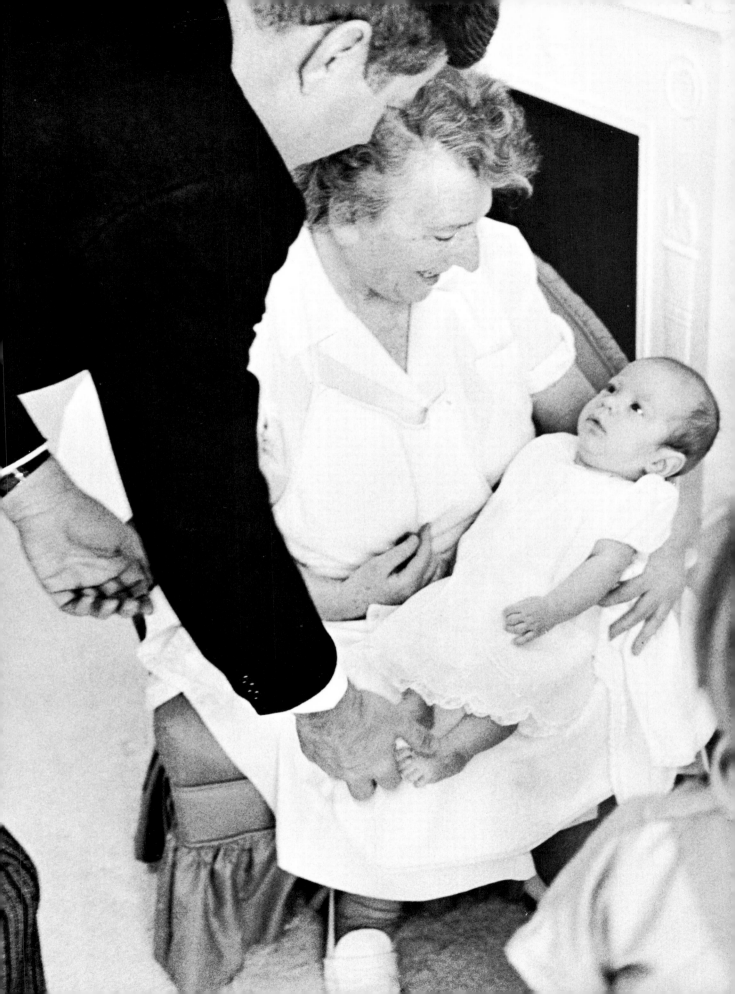

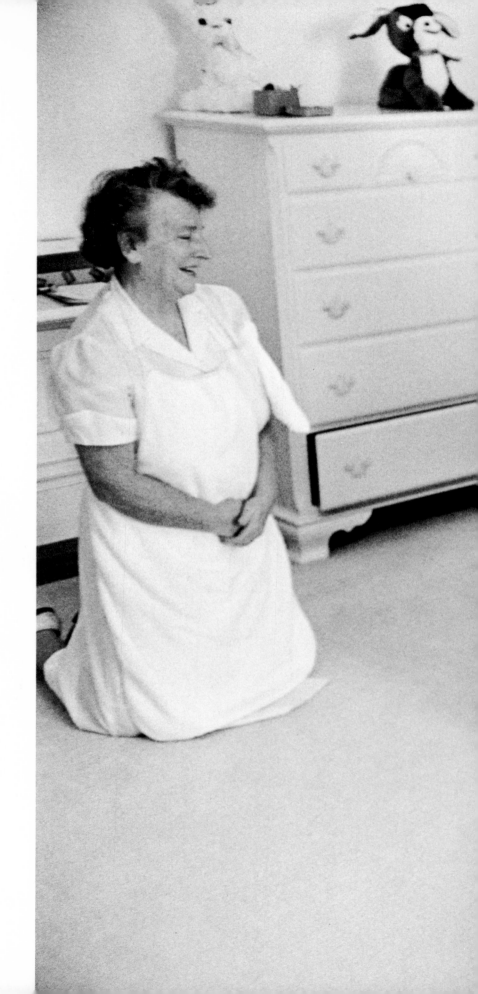

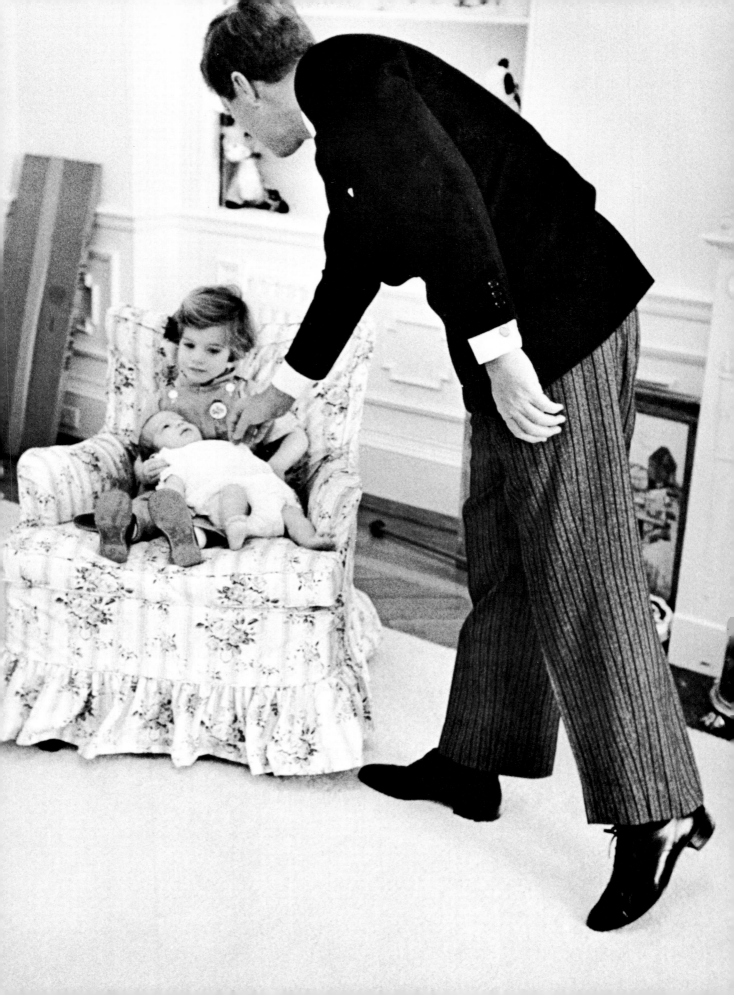

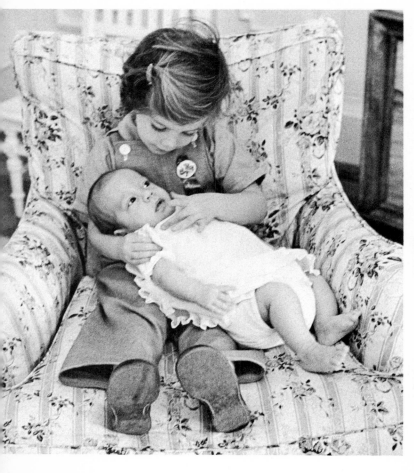

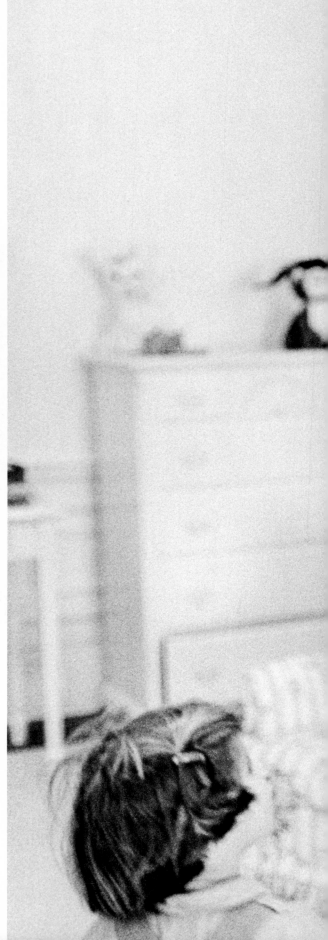

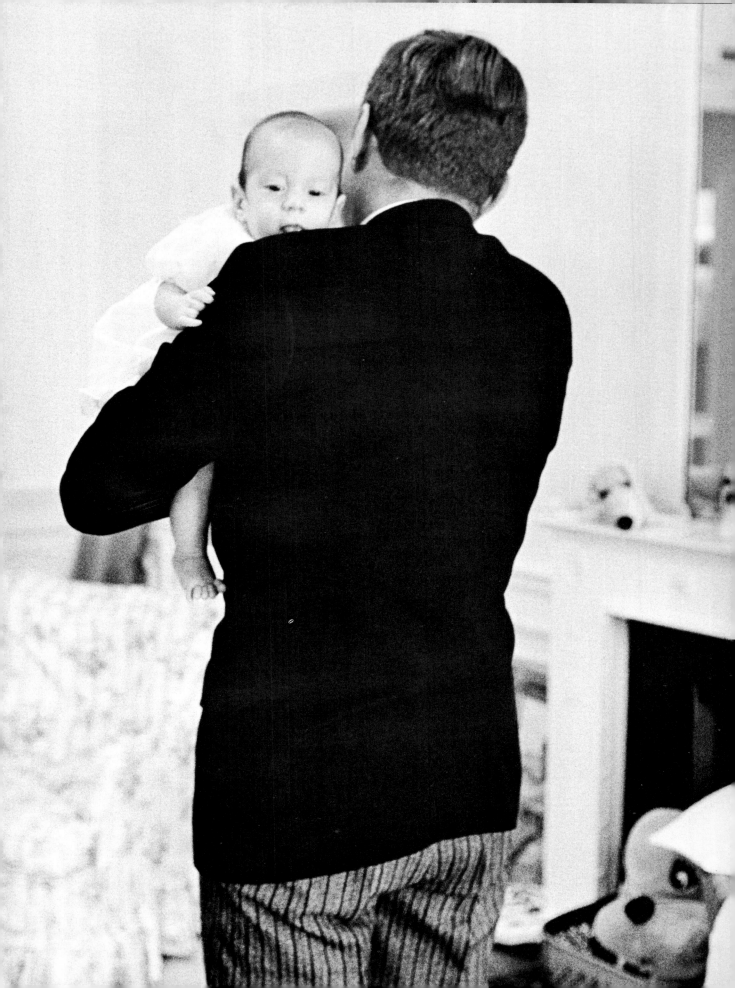

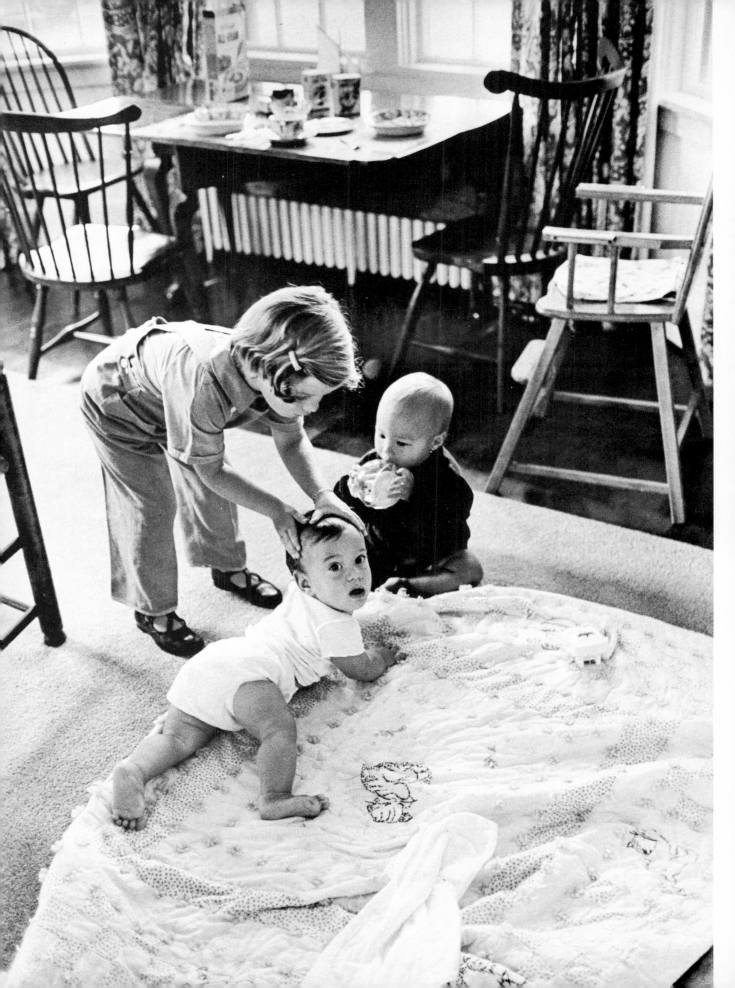

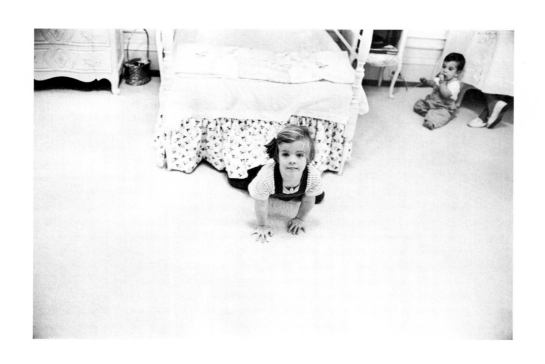

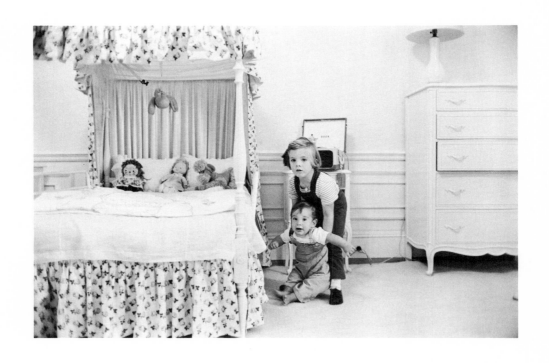

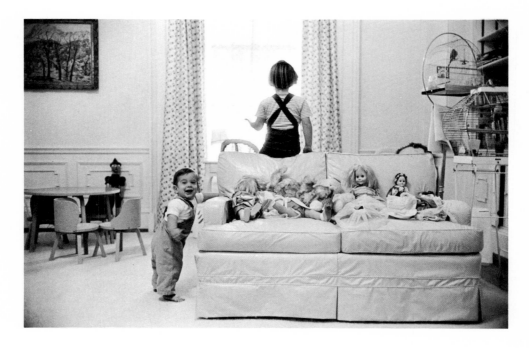

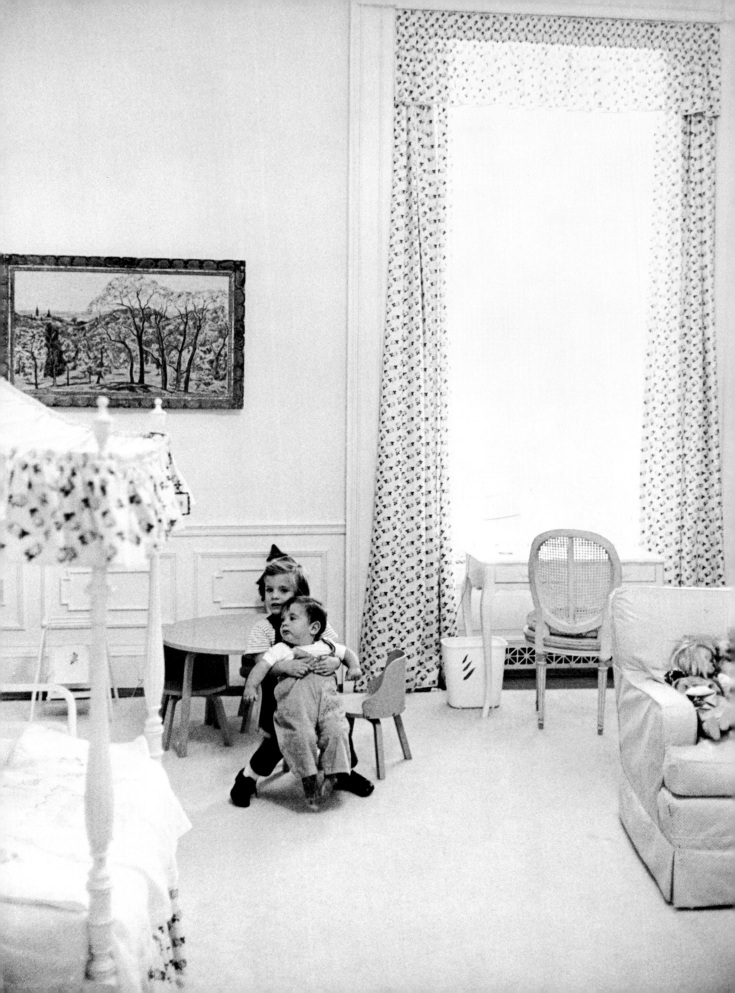

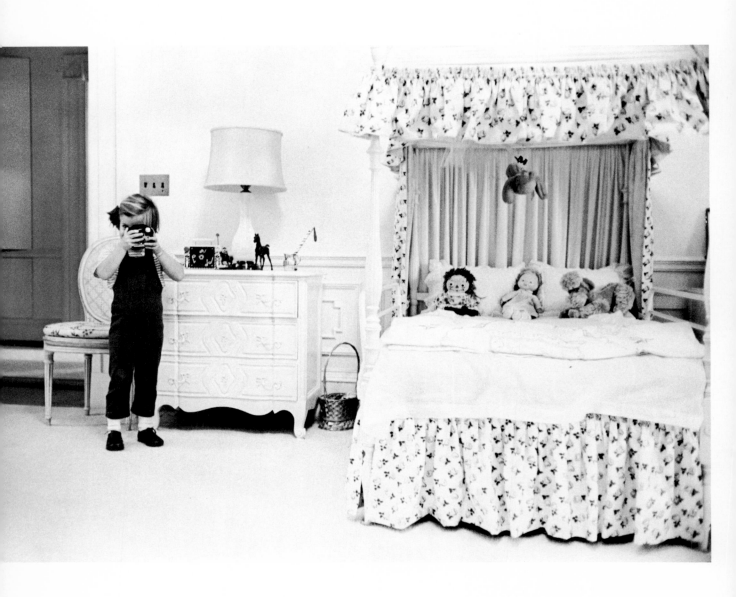

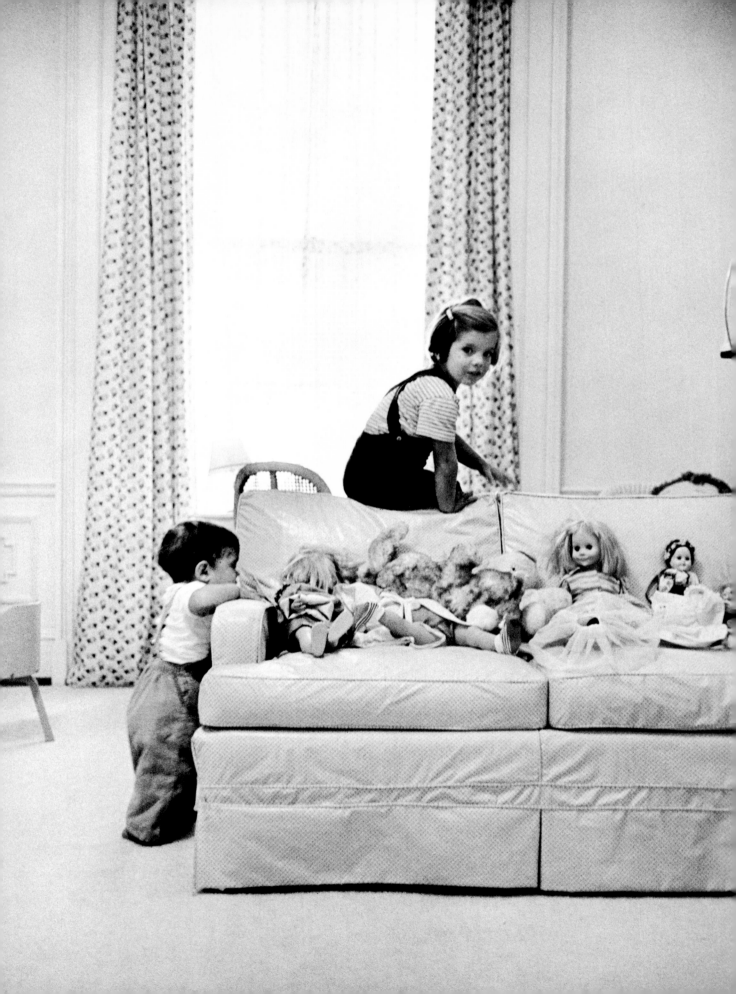

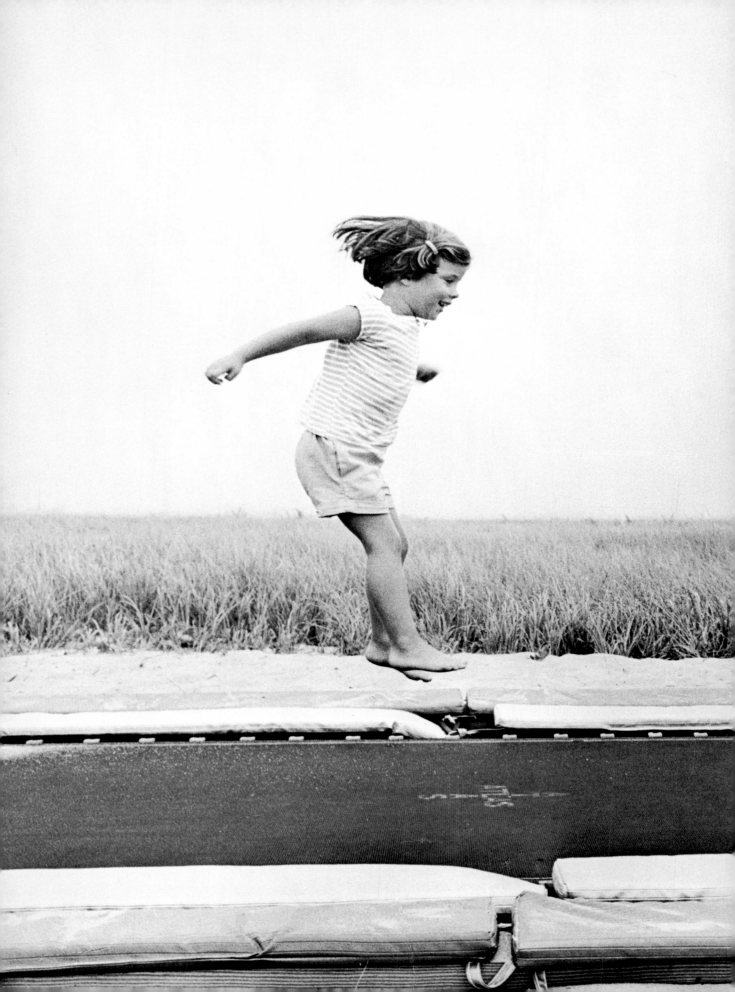

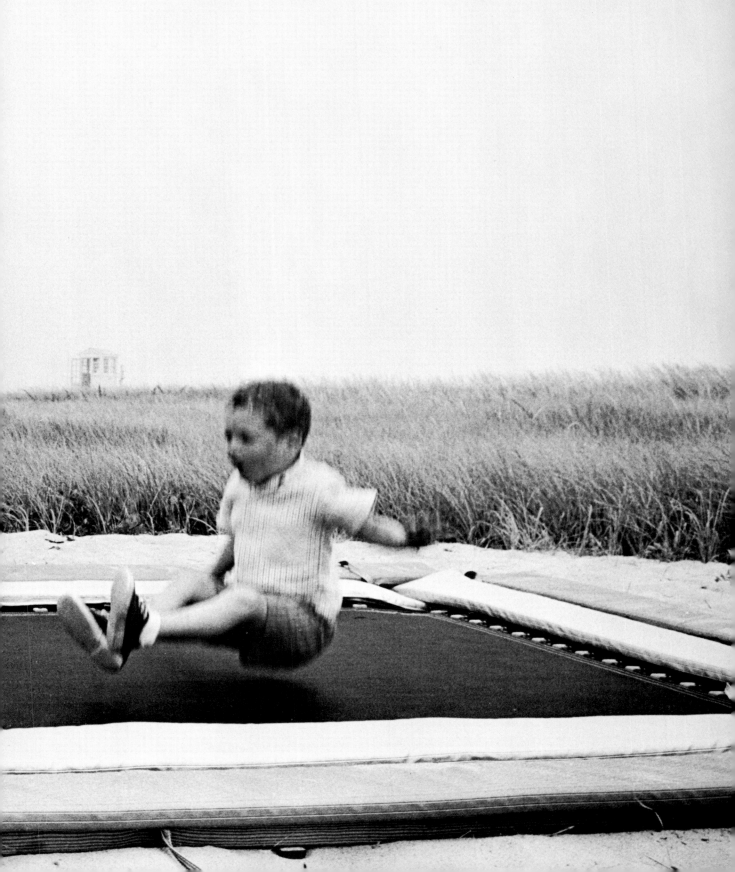

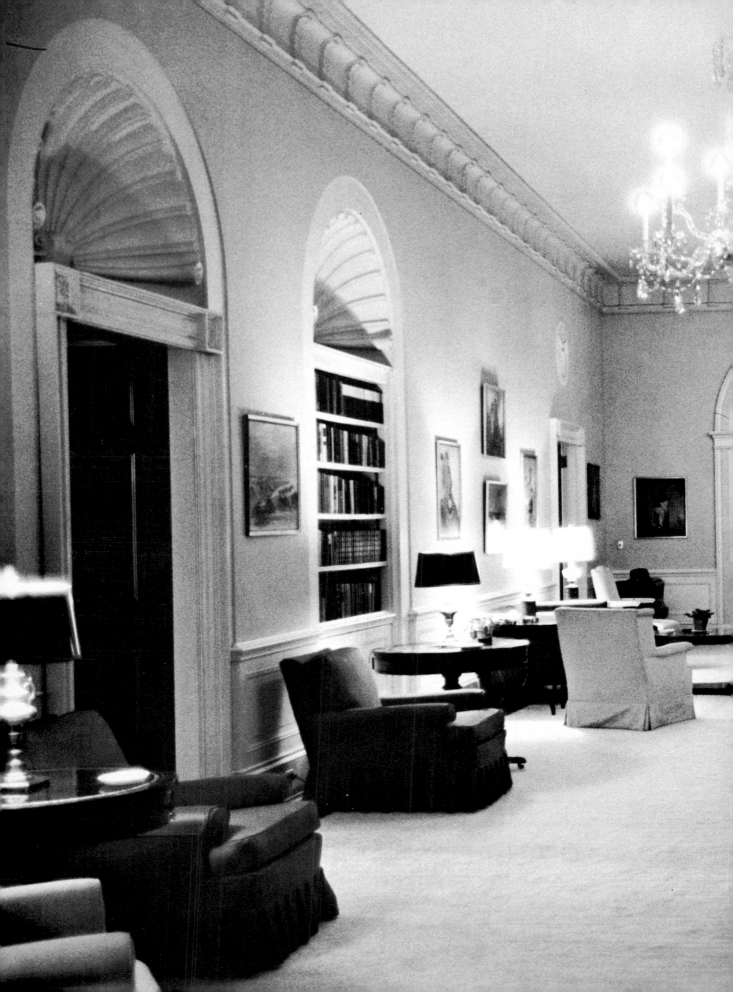

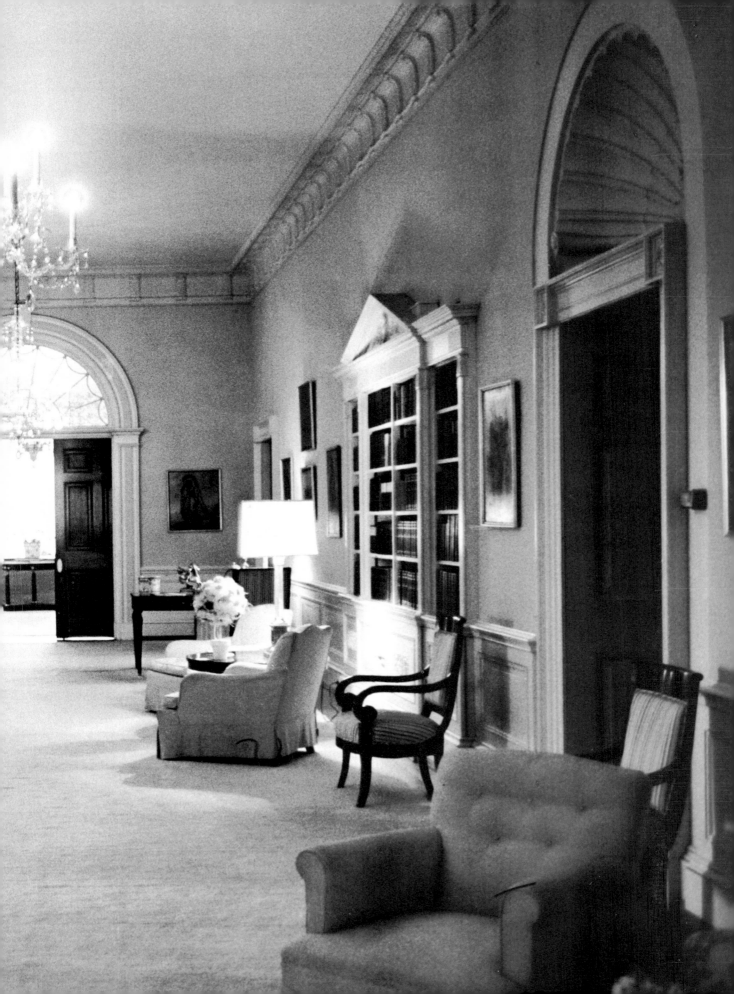

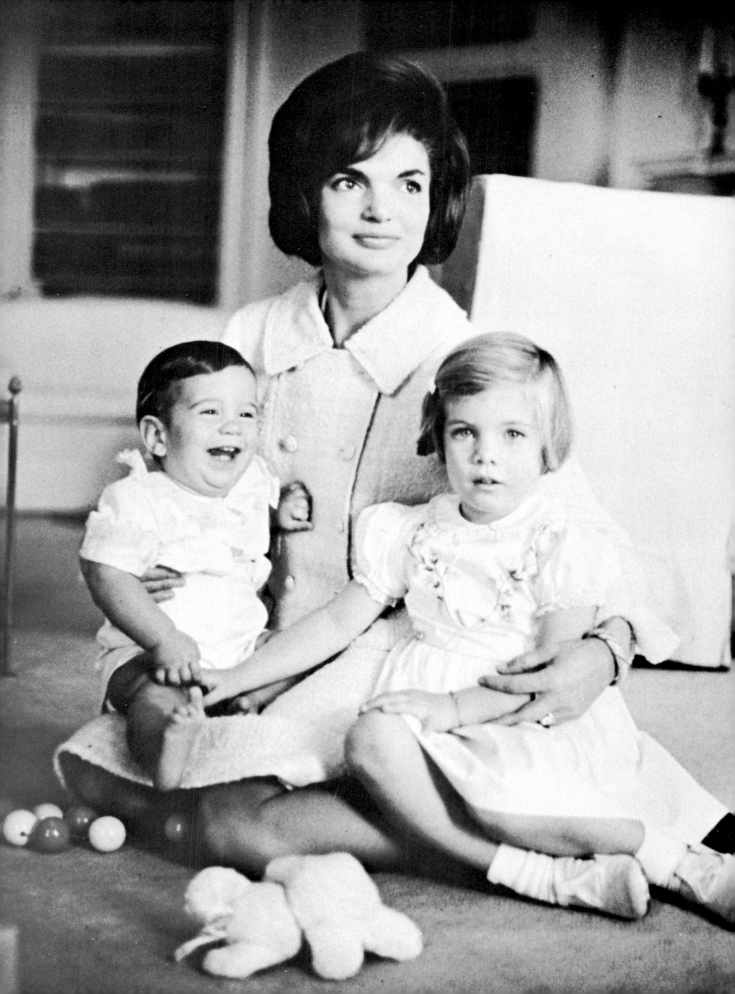

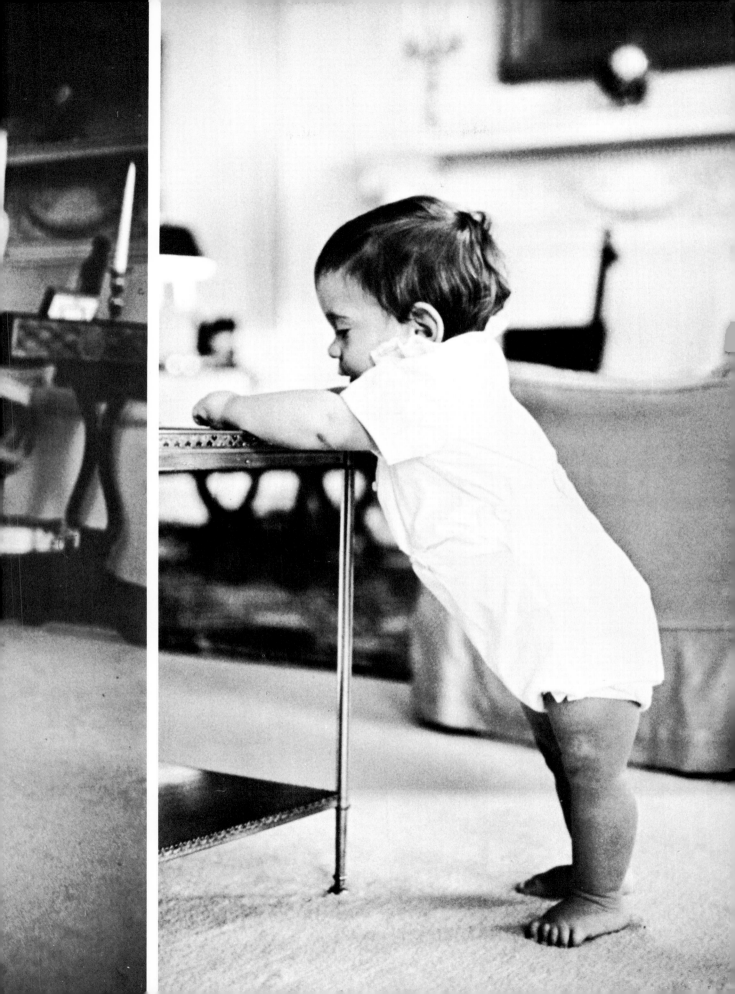

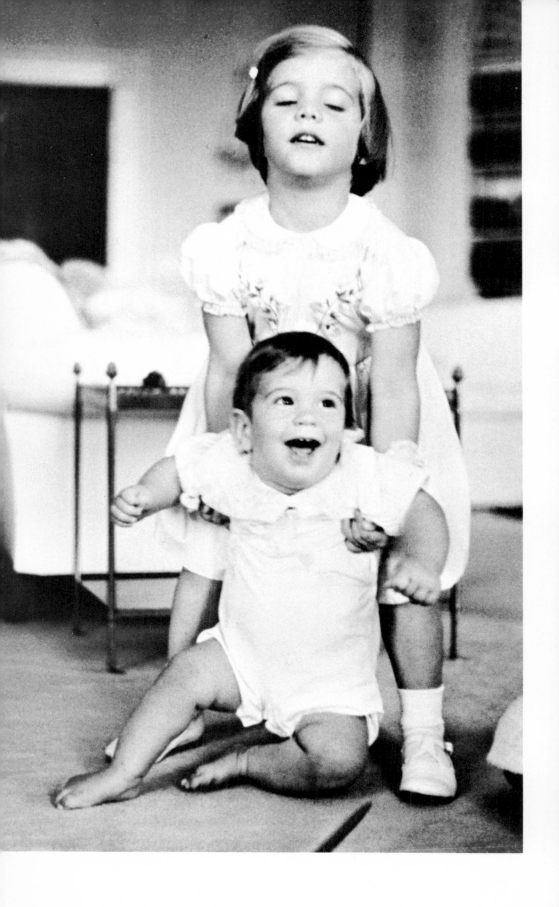
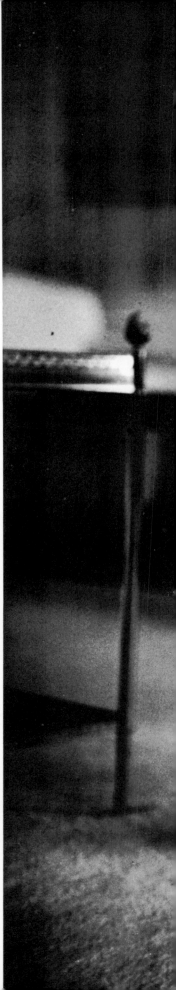

116

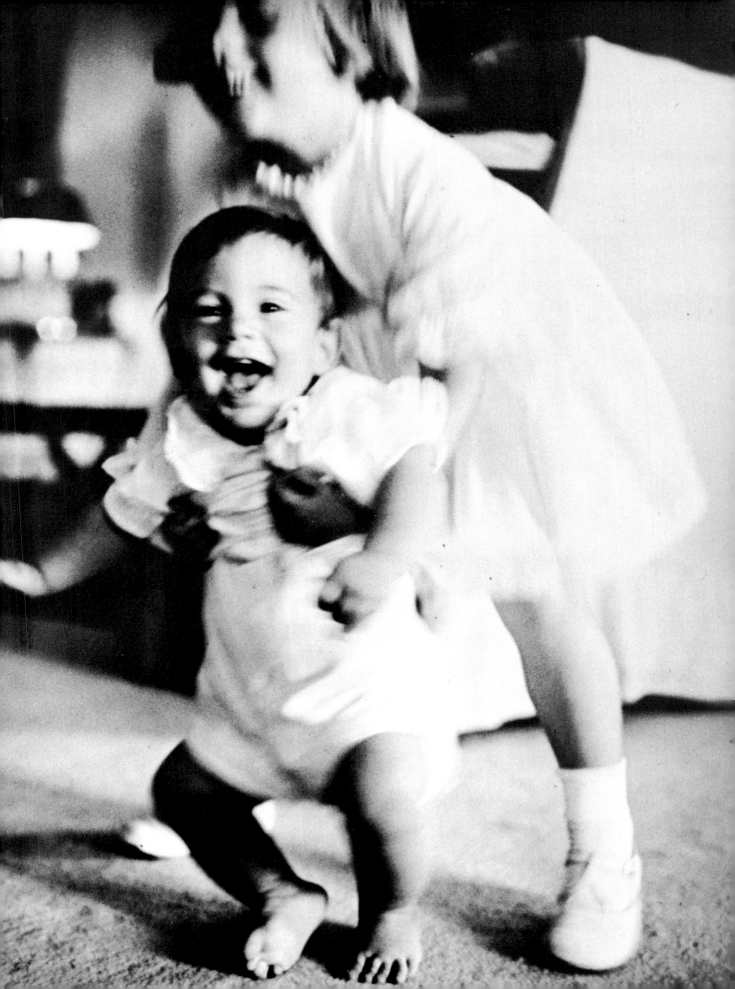

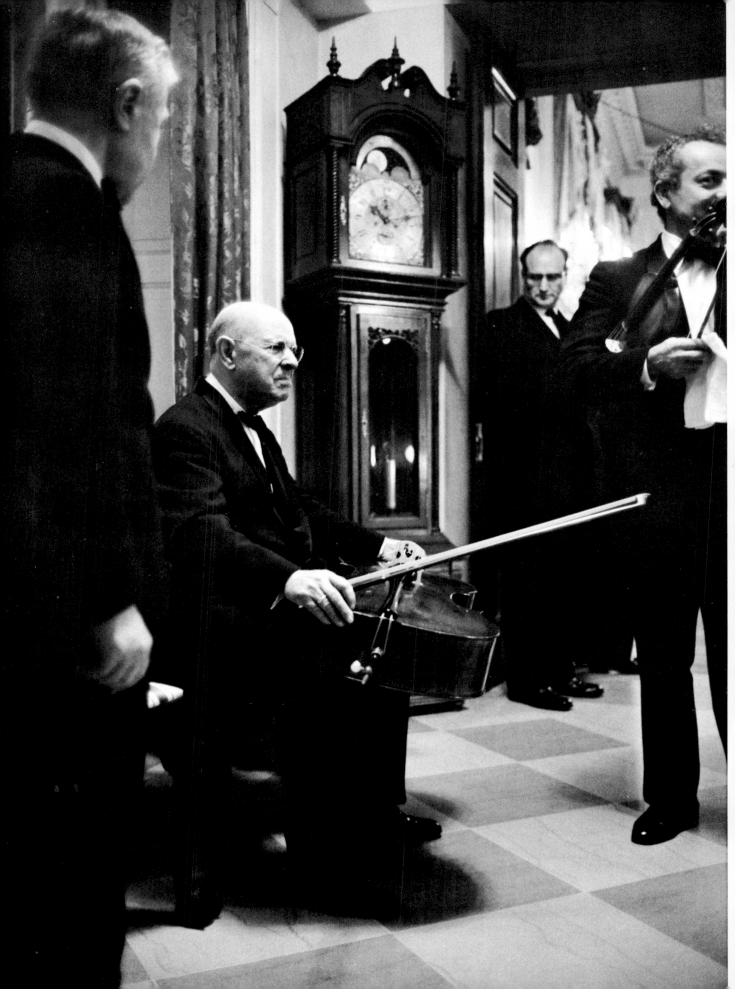

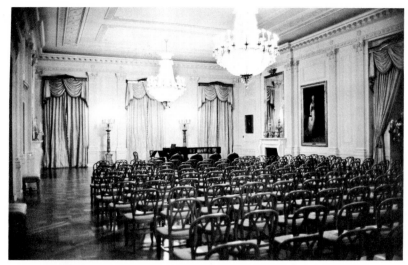

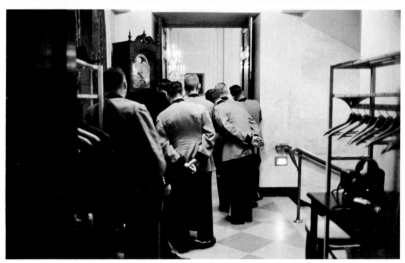

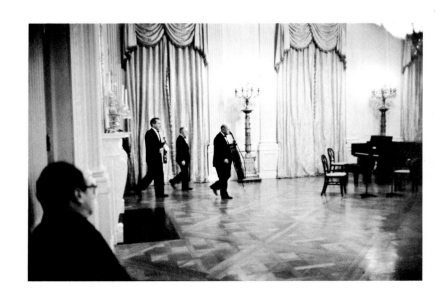

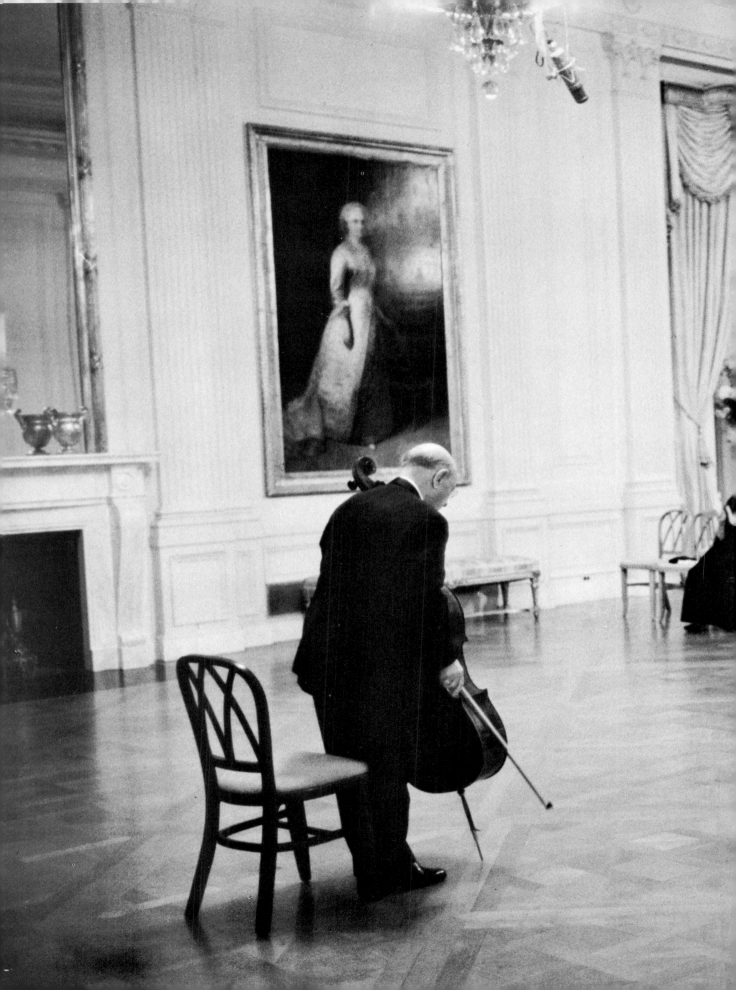

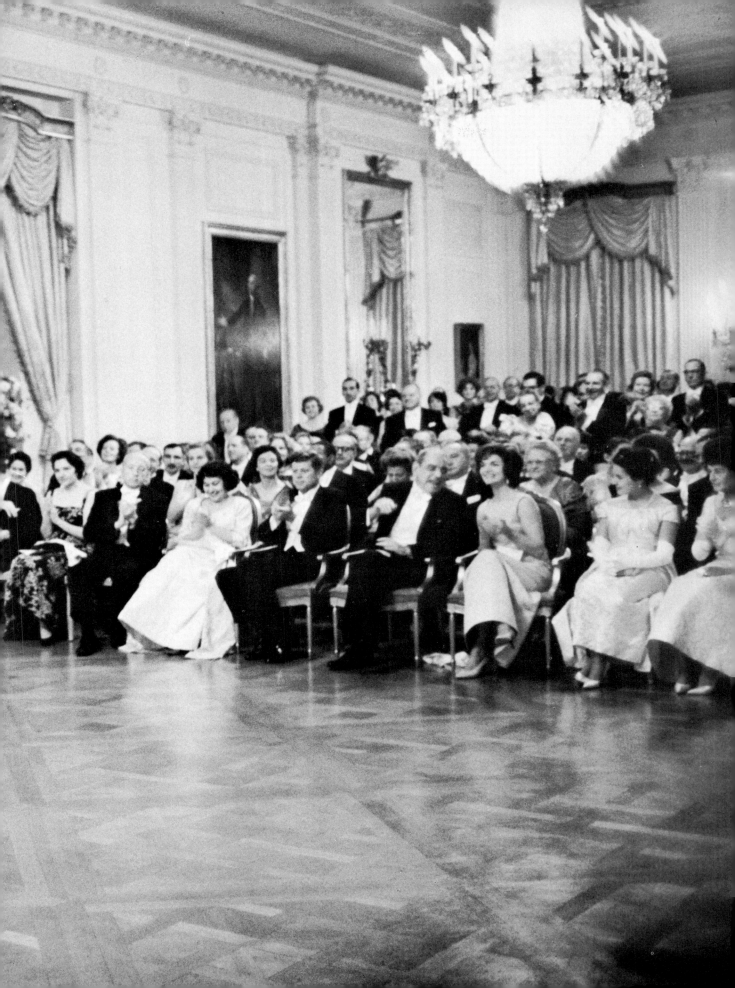

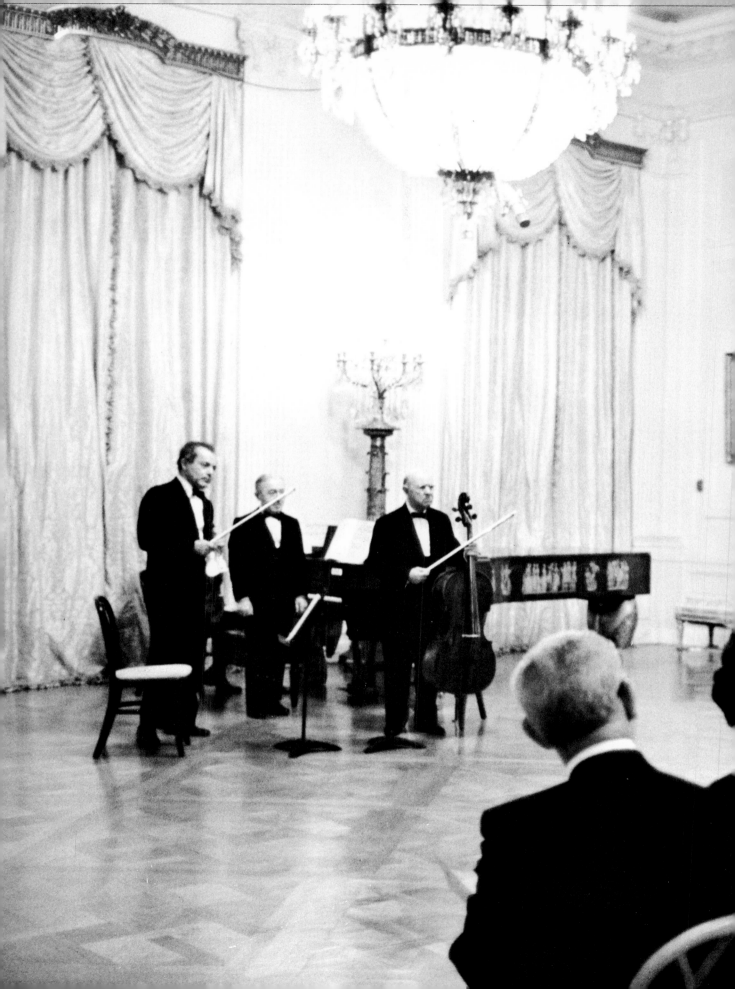

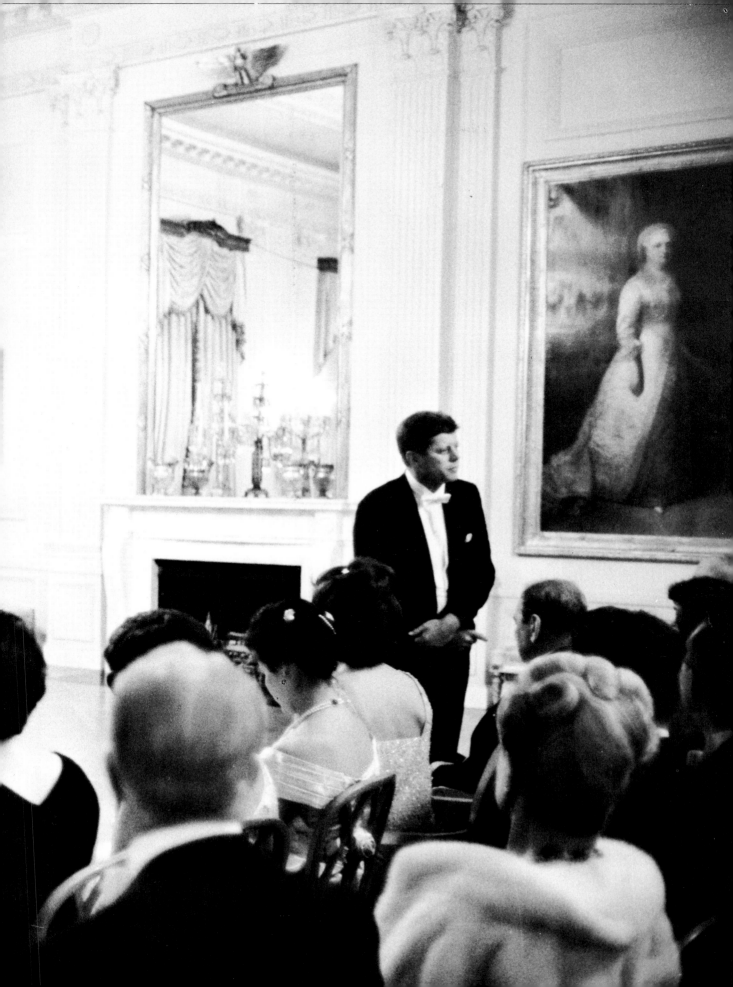

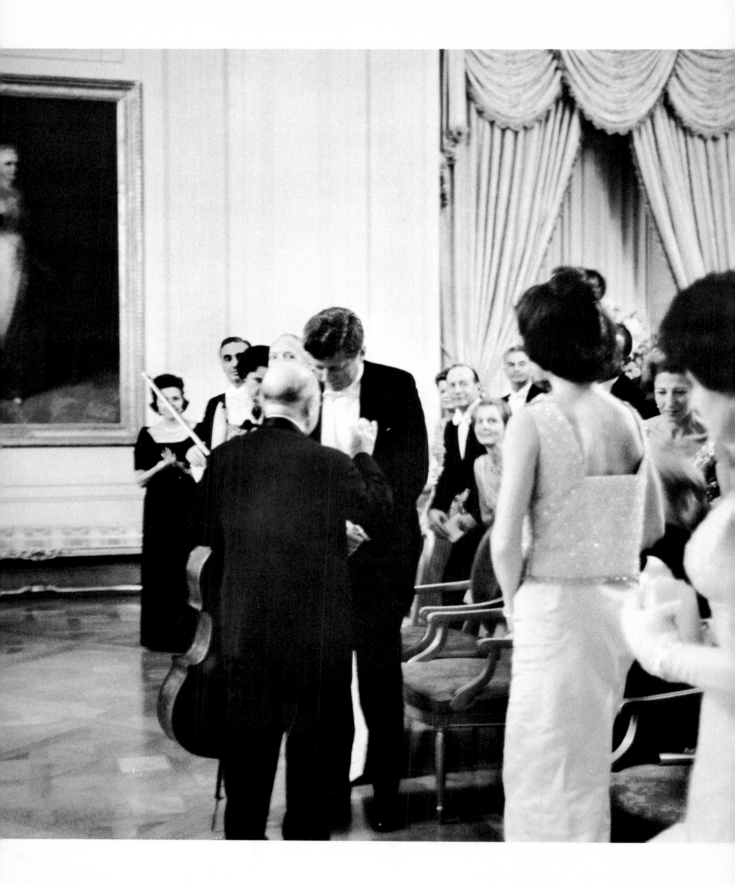

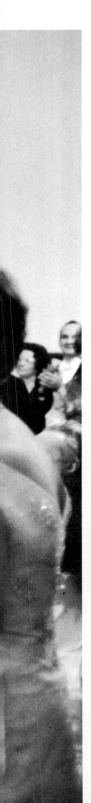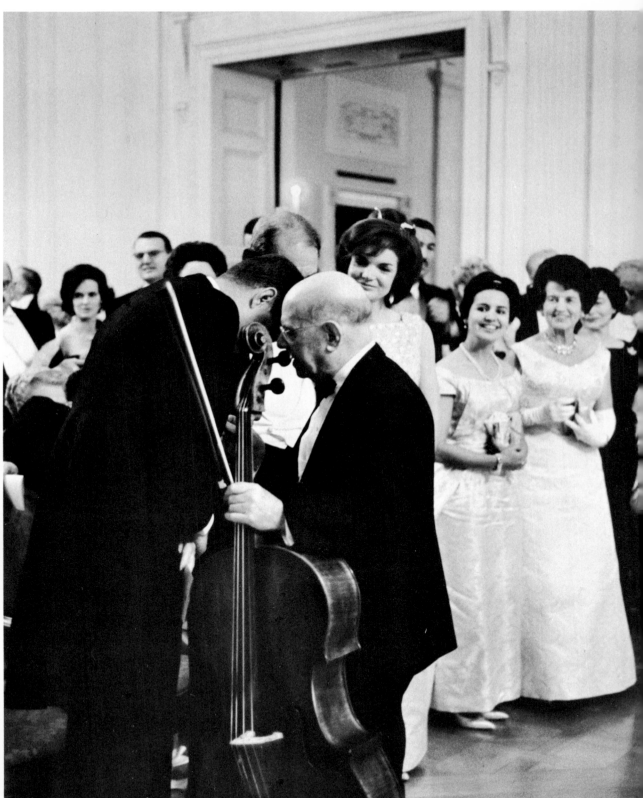

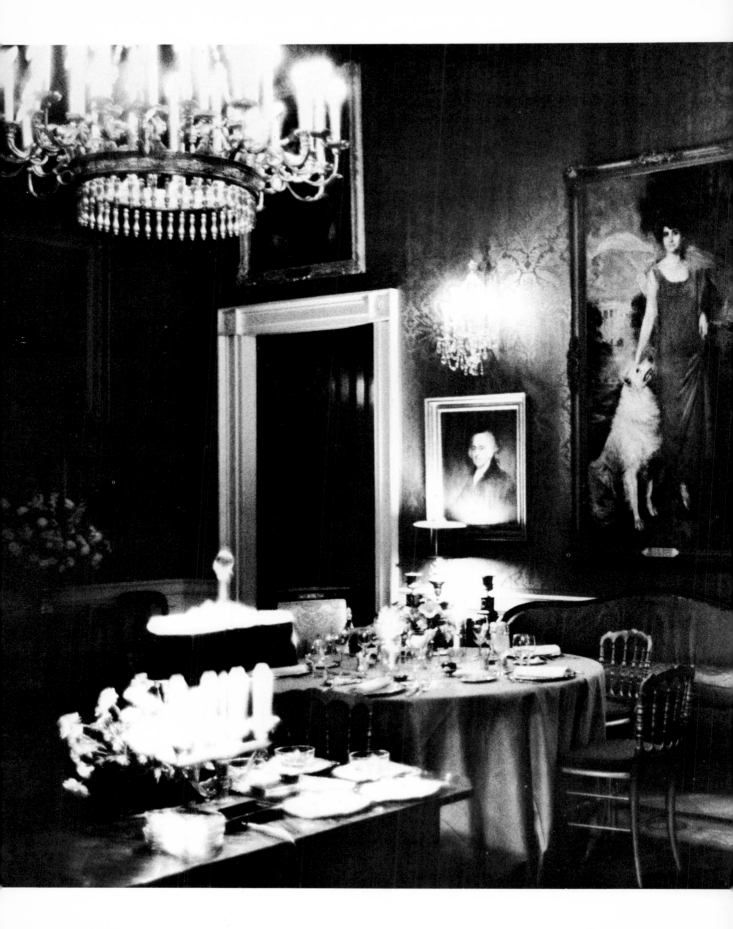

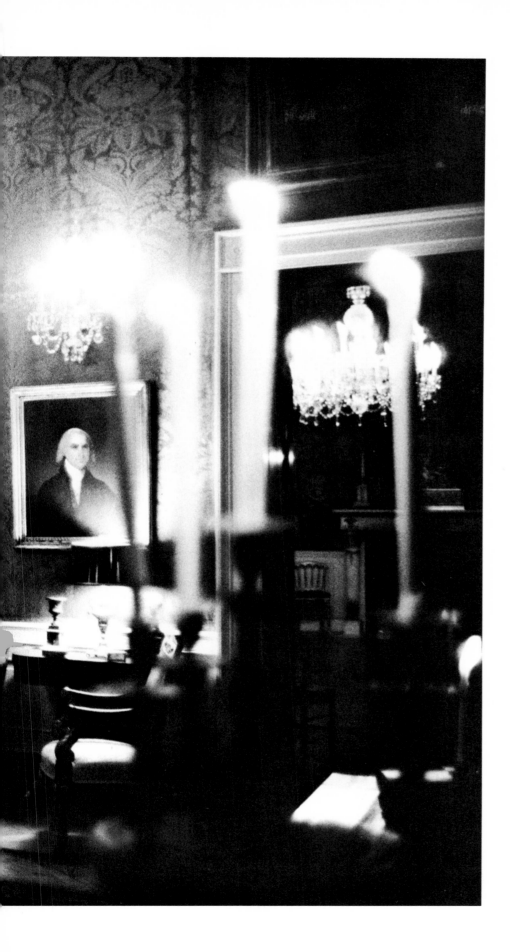

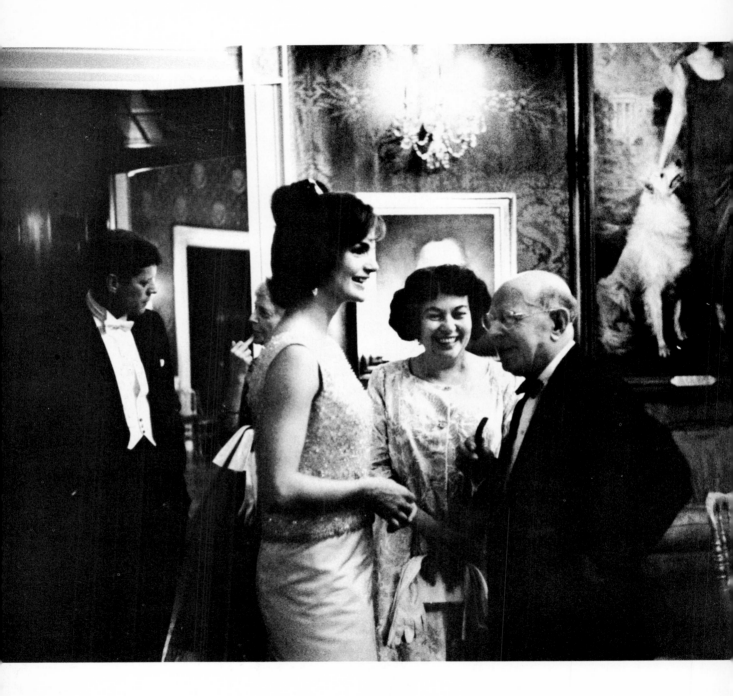

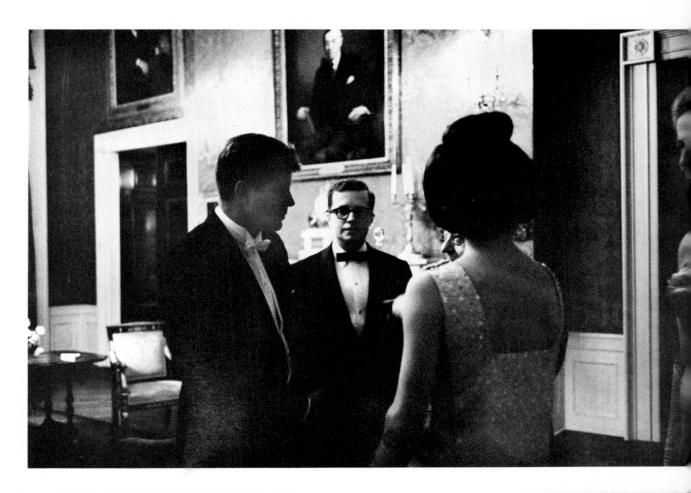

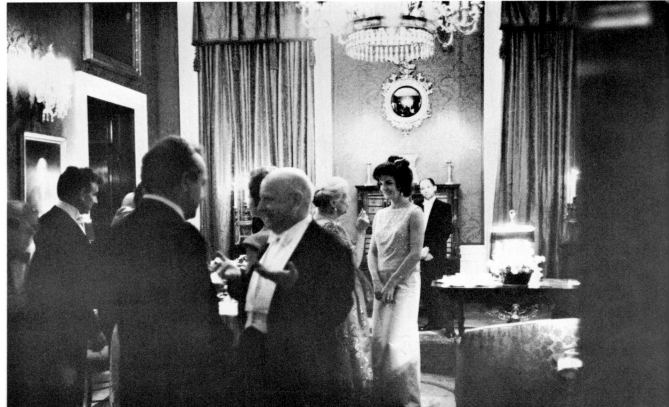

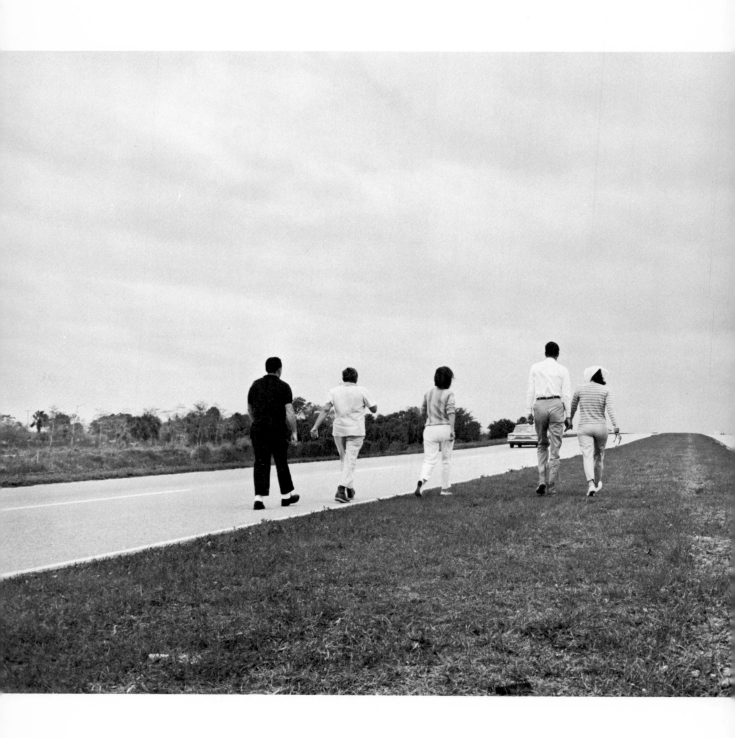

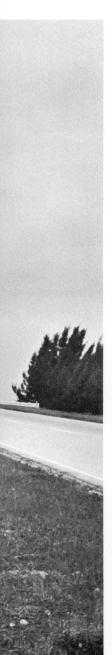

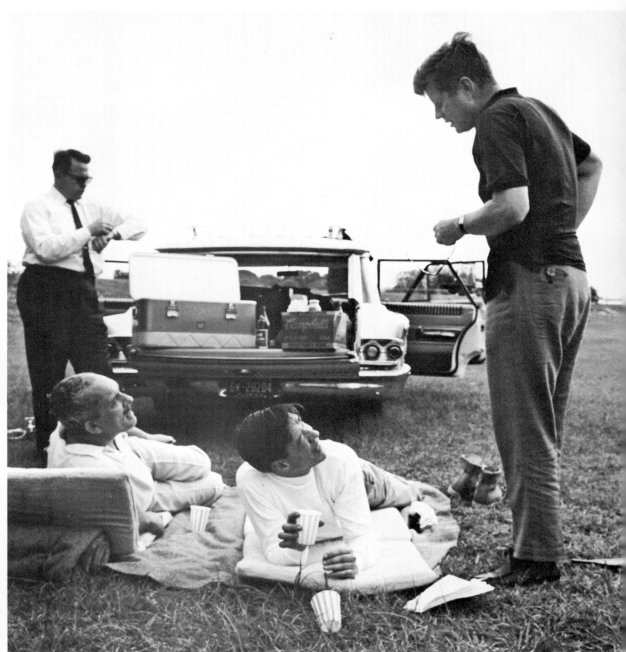

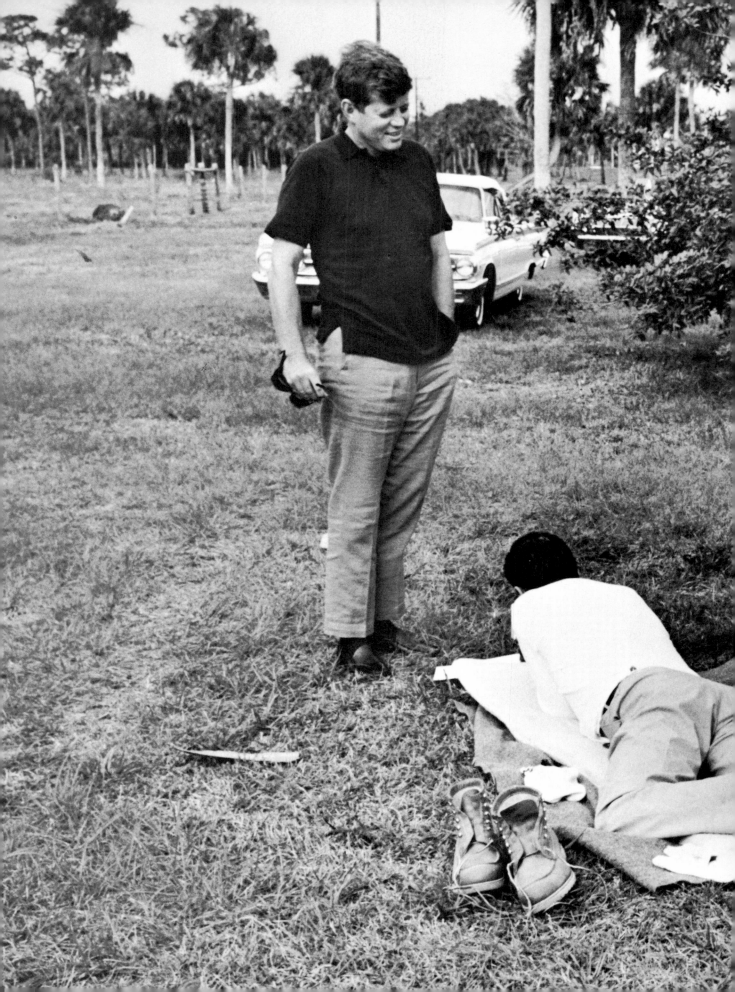

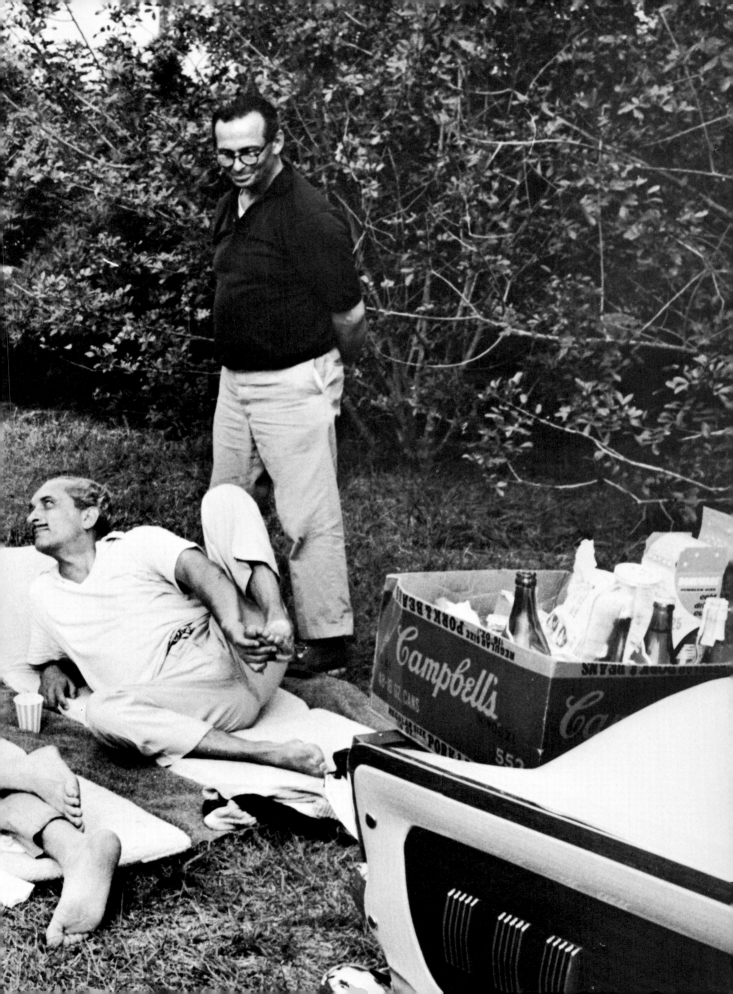

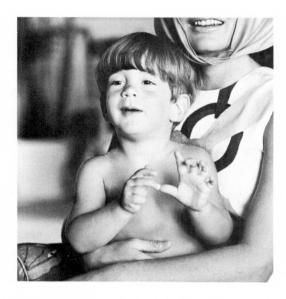

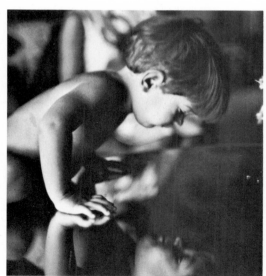

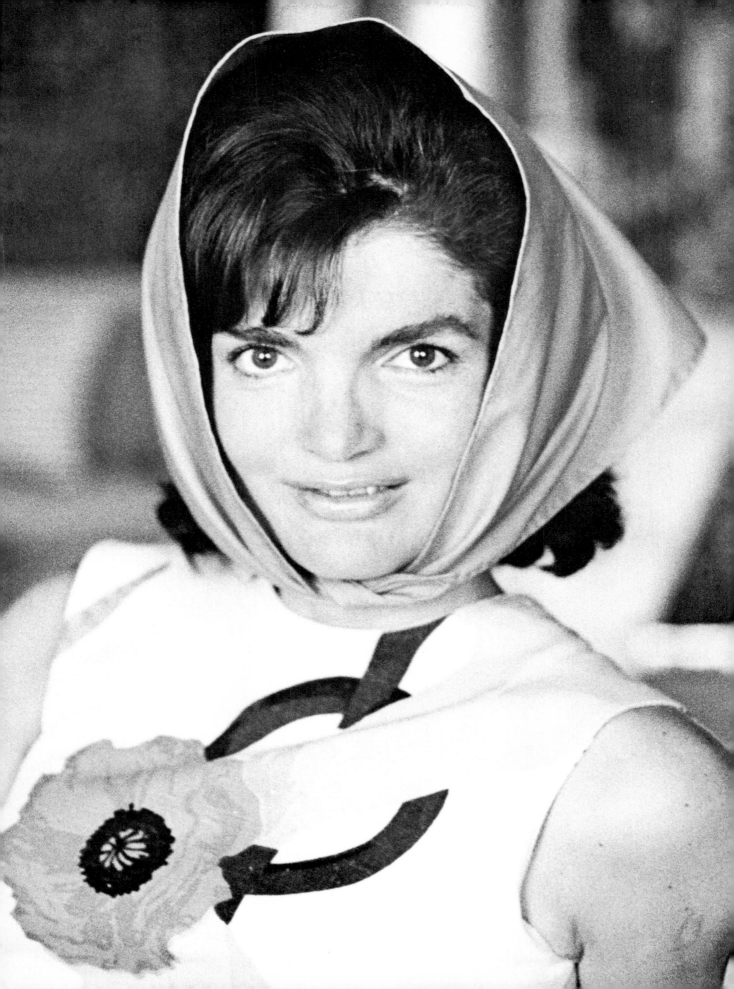

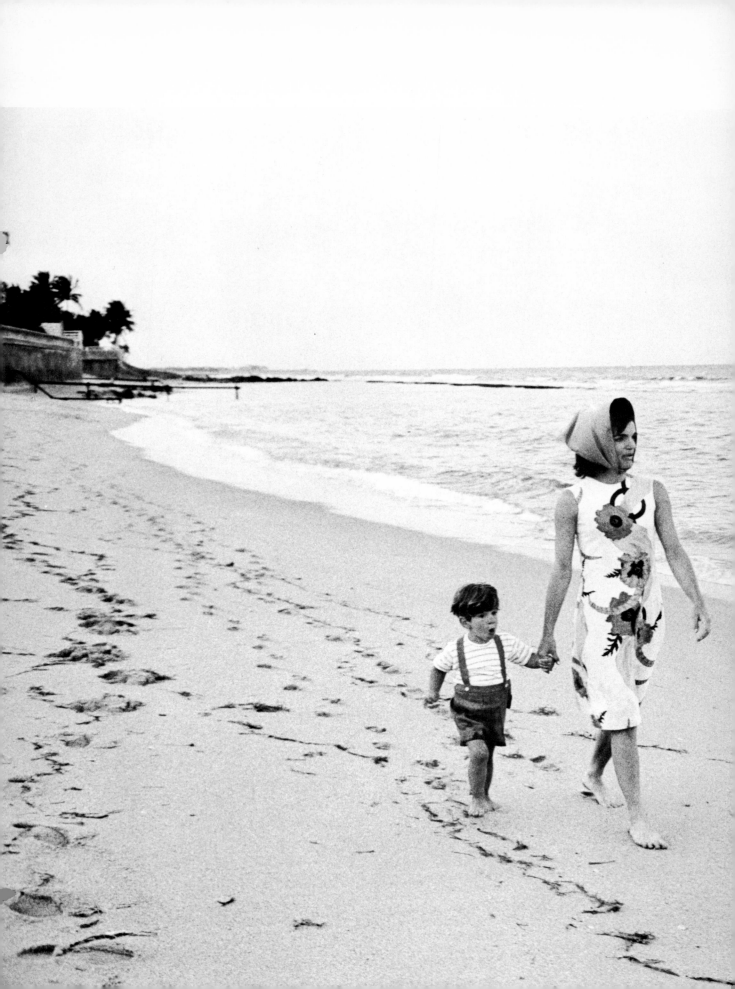

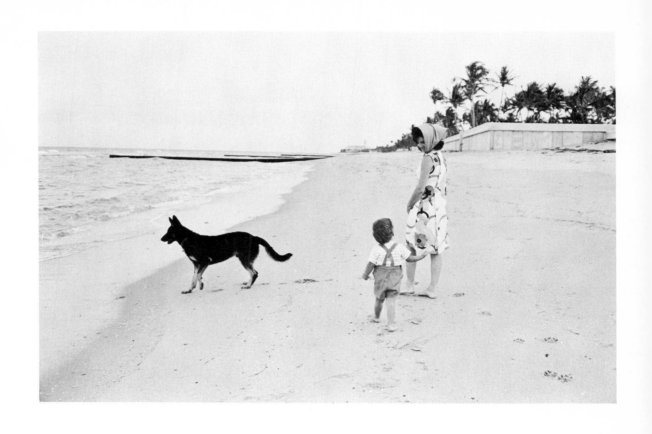

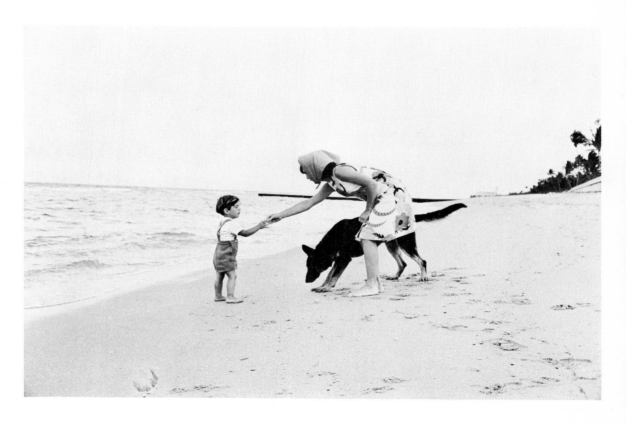

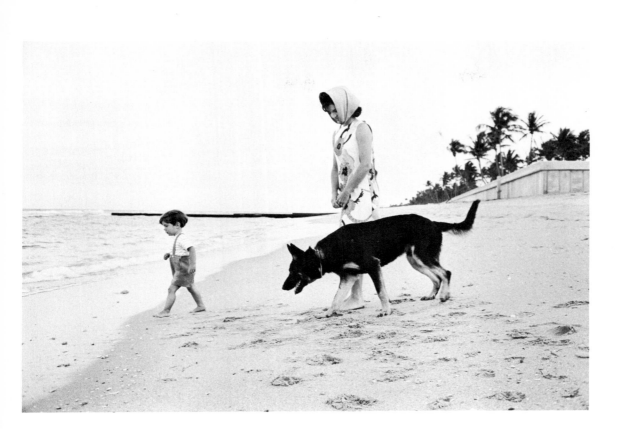

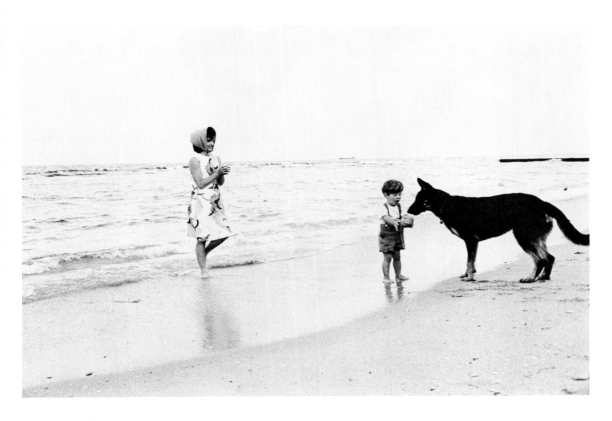

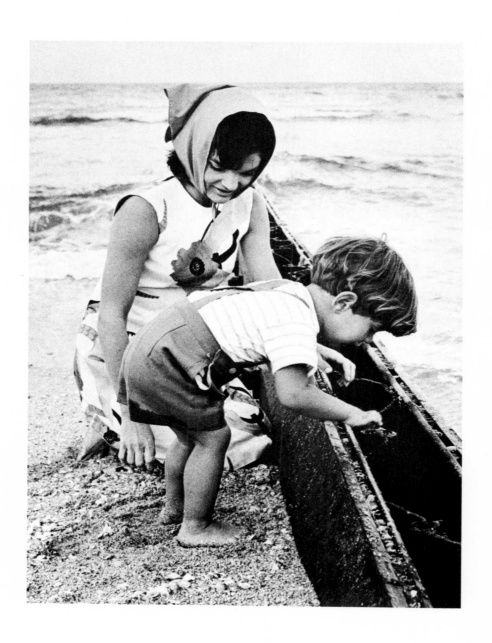

140

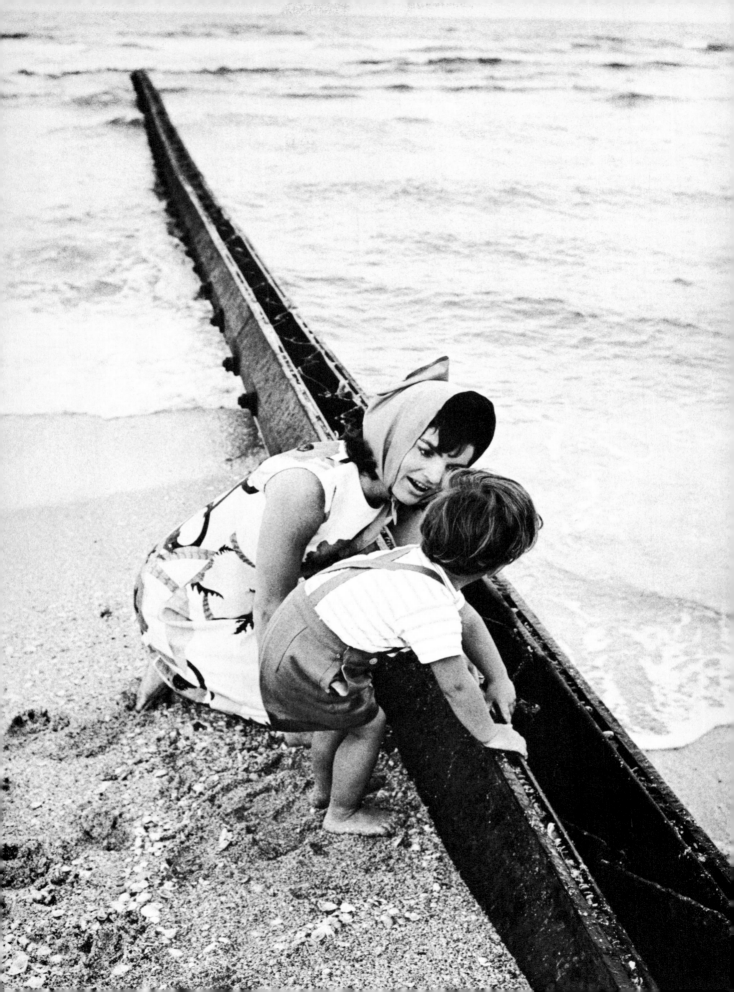

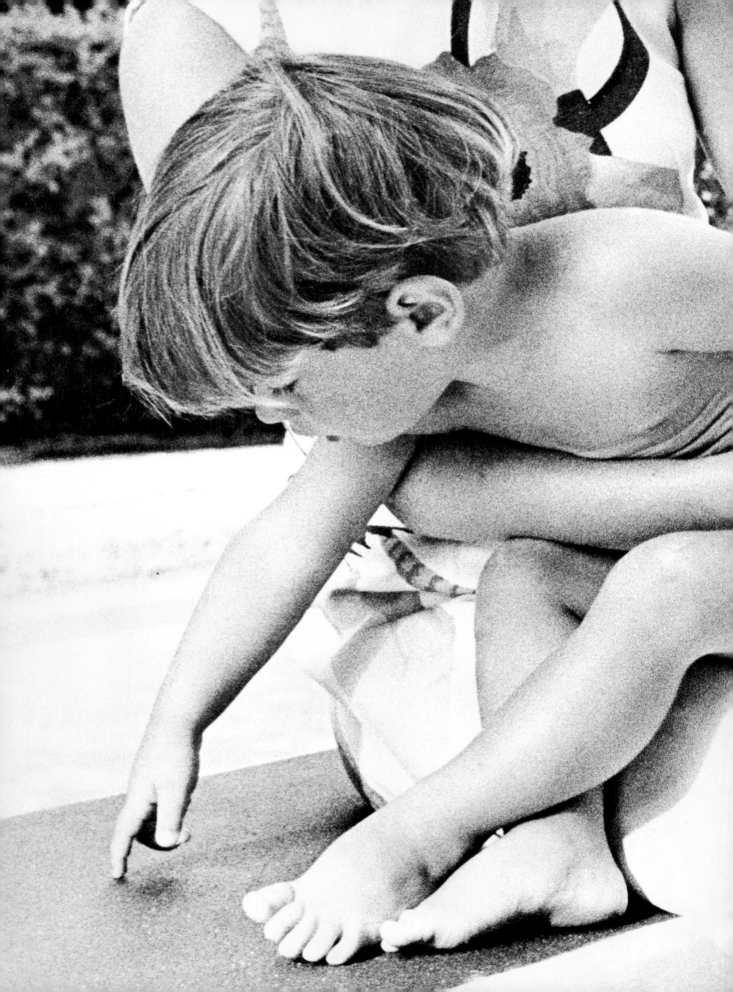

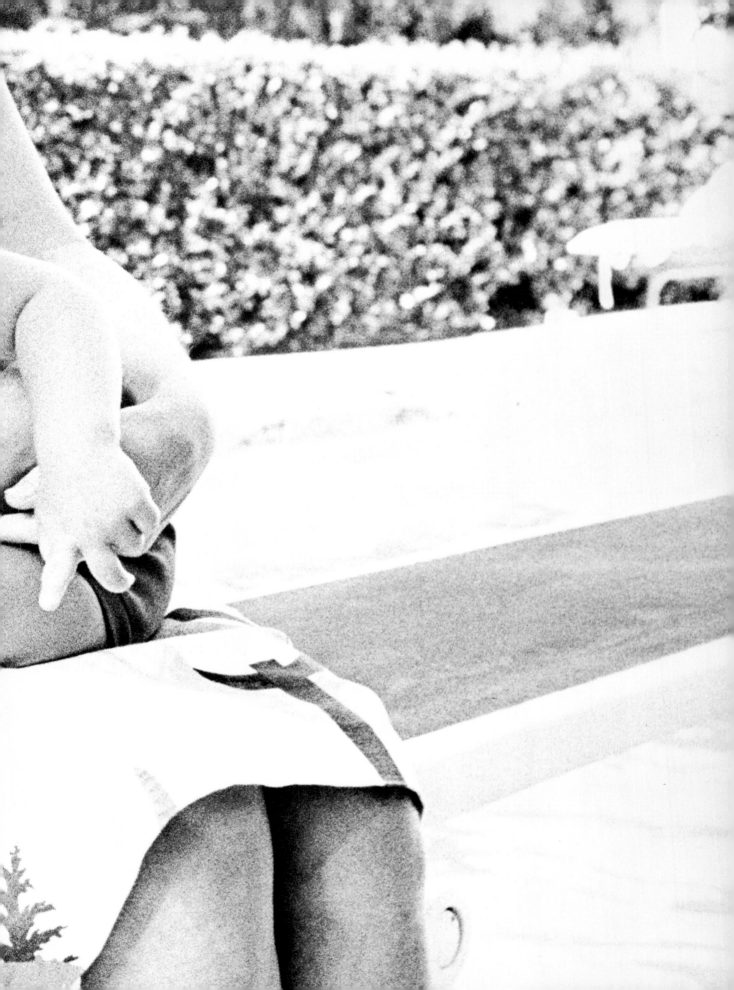

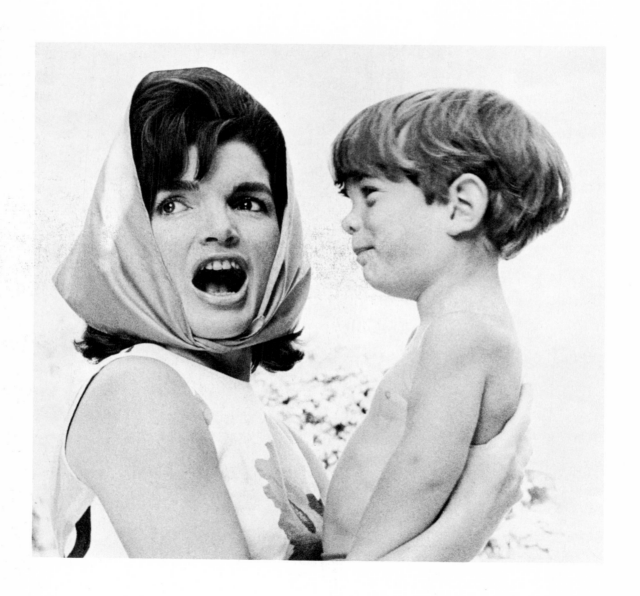

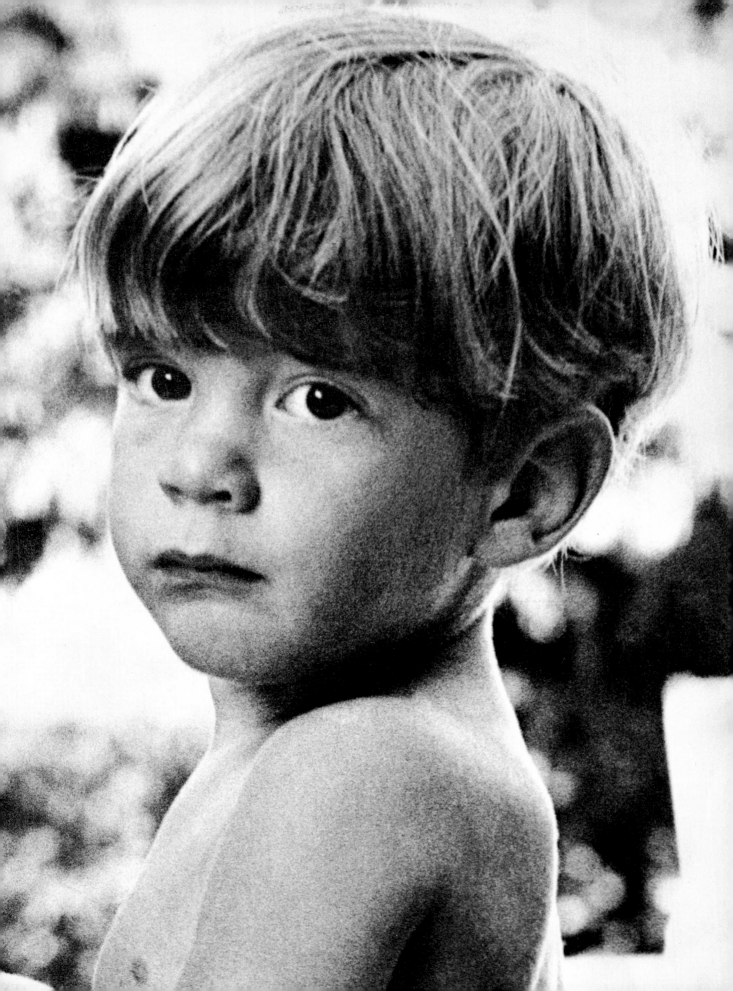

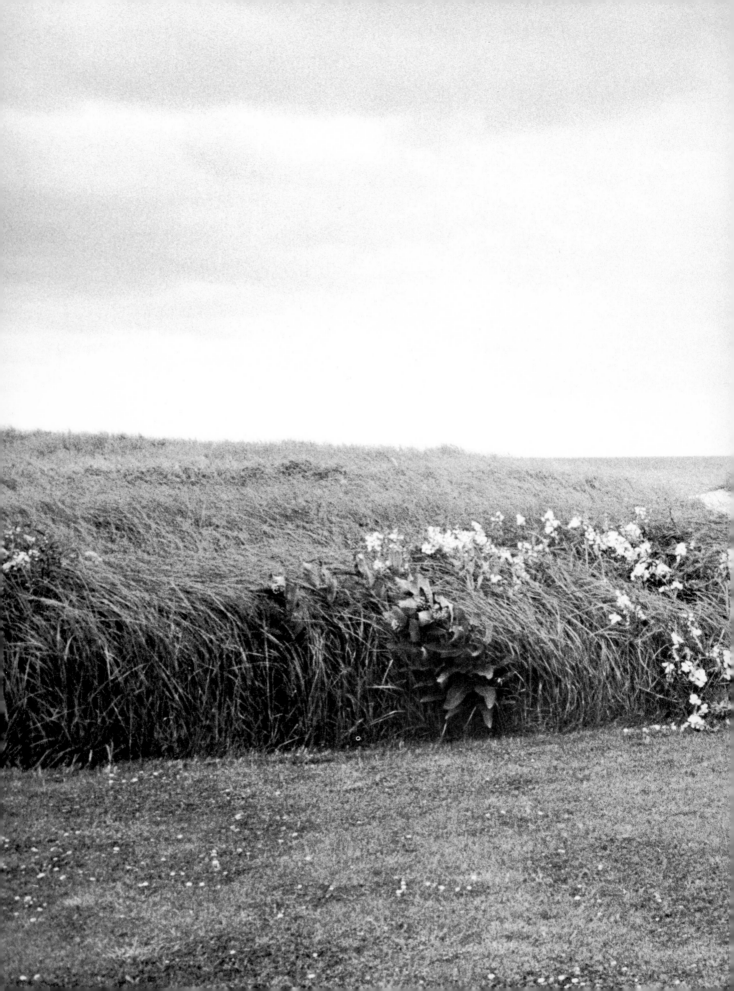

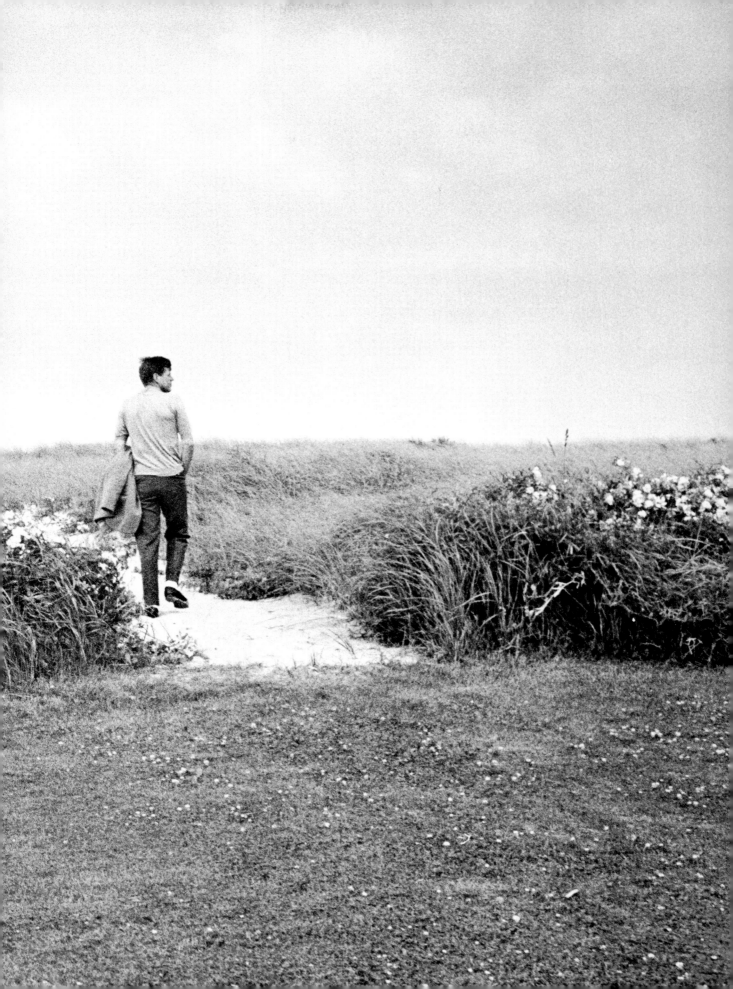

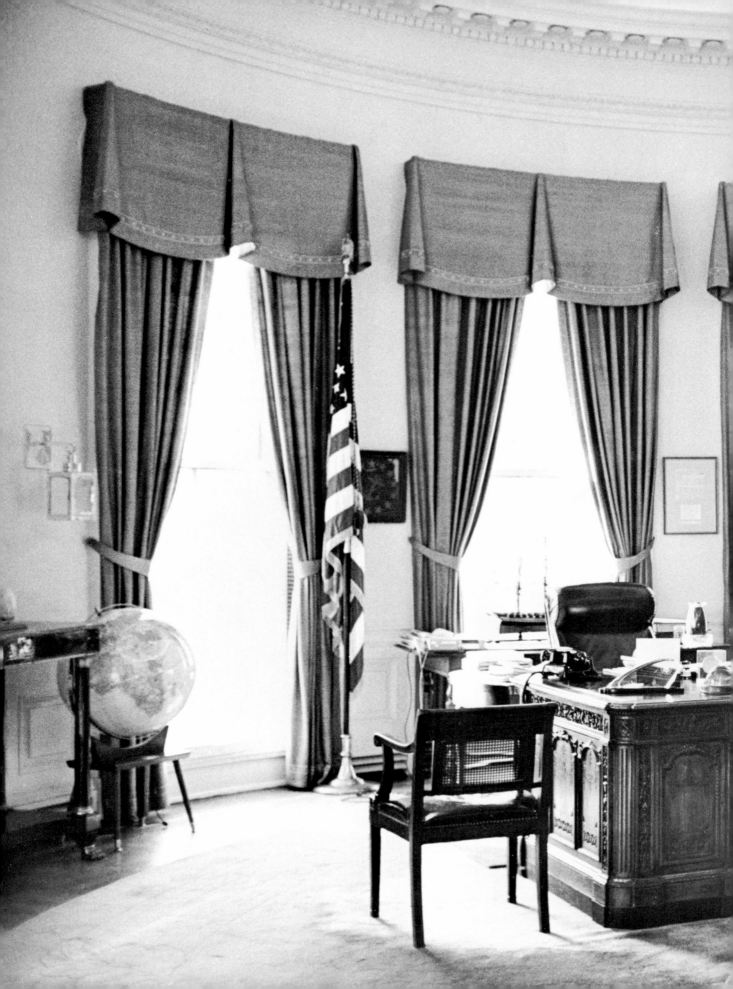

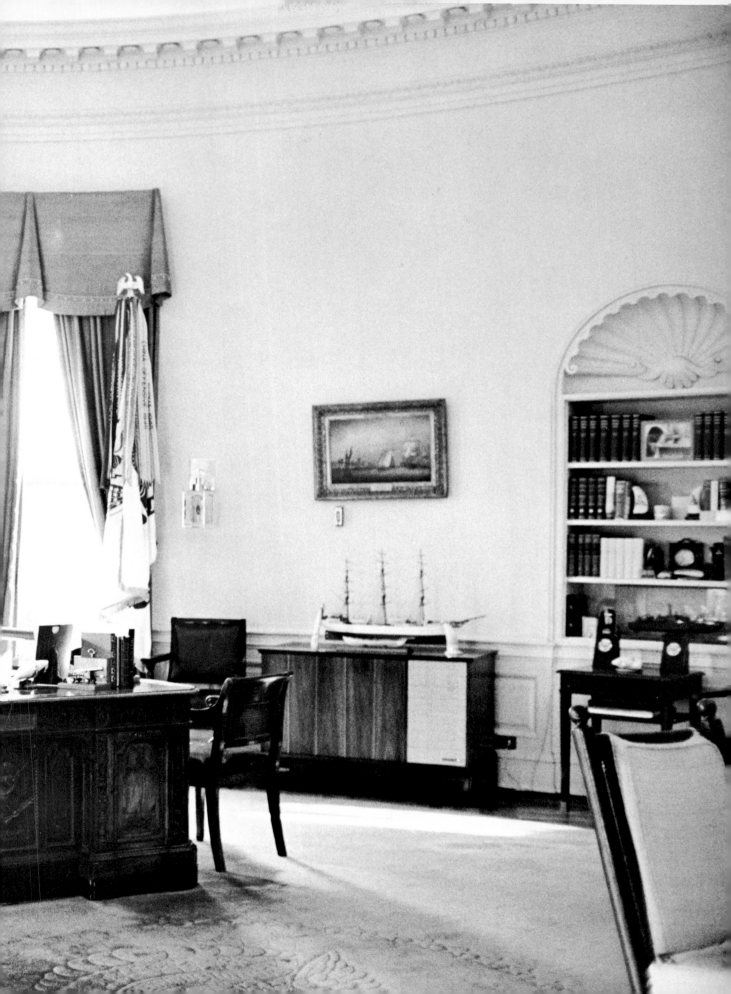

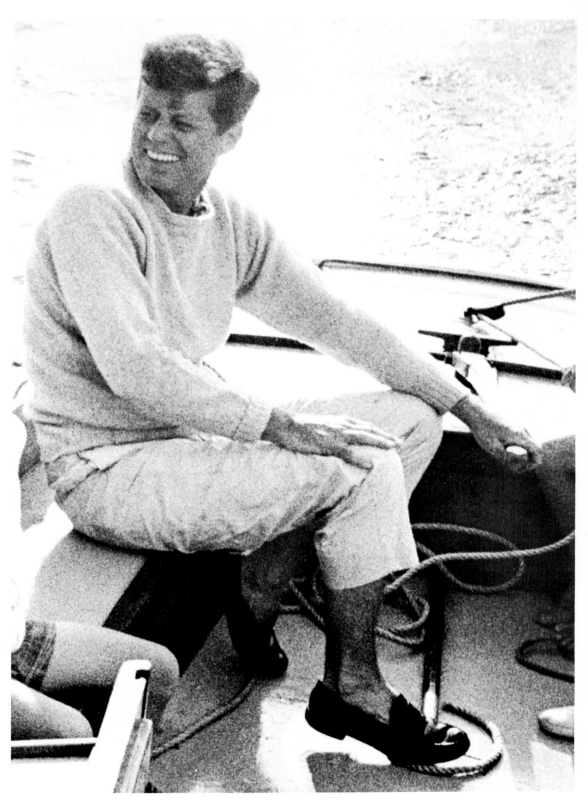

John Fitzgerald Kennedy
1917-1963

THIS BOOK IS DEDICATED TO MY FRIEND AND COMPANION
DR. MAX JACOBSON

ACKNOWLEDGMENTS

My deepest appreciation to:
Sam Sako, my faithful darkroom man, Trudy Owett, my personal
assistant, Clifford Wolf, my photographic assistant, and
the Studio personnel: R.O., D.W., M.B., M.O., V.H.

Robert Cato, who helped select the pictures and designed the book.

The editors of *Life,* who gave me the initial assignment to
photograph John F. Kennedy.

And most of all my wife Pat Suzuki, who through the years gave
me the encouragement and time to prepare this book.

Some of the photographs in this book have appeared in *Life,*
Ladies' Home Journal, McCall's and *Redbook.* The pictures on
pages 29, 52-53, 90 and 146-147 were first published in *Vogue.*

Notes on the Photographs in This Book

This book is not intended to be a complete photographic record or documentary of the John F. Kennedy family. The pictures are not in chronological order and I have avoided supplying specific dates, because with few exceptions the day or event was not important. For the most part these photographs are not of state occasions or ceremonies, nor do they show moments of crisis or violence. These photographs were taken in order to catch and reflect the mood, the feeling of a given moment. If the viewer receives from these pictures an understanding of the affection of the Kennedys for one another, their high spirits and enjoyment of life, the book will have fulfilled its purpose.

M.S.

Title page: Hyannis Port in the fall of the year. The children are Robert Kennedy's.

Opening page: An official picture, never used, taken at the time of the Bay of Pigs disaster. The President later commented that he had decided not to release it. "I looked too serious." It was a grim, tense day, but he brought none of this to the top floor of the White House. Afterward he had lunch, a sandwich and fruit on a small tray. He made no mention of the cause and reason for his quiet.

The sailing series: Taken off Hyannis Port in the fall. Sunny days and after a round of golf everyone raced to the end of the dock and went sailing. It was the practice that before the Kennedy children could sail, they would be thrown overboard in the open sea with life preservers so that they wouldn't panic when they later had an accidental plunge.

Next two double-page pictures: Late afternoon on the back lawn of Joseph Kennedy's house in Hyannis Port. One was always aware of the three family houses facing the tree-covered street. In front, leaves on the ground; in back, the gently rolling lawn down to the Atlantic Ocean. I was most conscious of the flow of children — the area was later aptly called the "Compound." Clothes were casual. A strong bent for the active life and also an intense life of reading, discussion of current events, and general awareness.

Strolling through the back of Robert Kennedy's house. Underneath, the children running and showering. Never the feeling of pressure or time.

Following page 21: Georgetown, the last weeks before election. Breakfast early but leisurely, time to read the paper and talk and play with the children. After J.F.K. left for the Senate Office Building, Jackie would stay around the house until later in the morning, when she usually took a walk by the Georgetown canal.

Dinner at Georgetown with Senator and Mrs. John Sherman Cooper. George the butler.

The Senate office, just before election.

Page 38 and following: Wheeling, West Virginia, a real pressure point. In the first picture are some of the people who surrounded Senator Kennedy in the early days of the campaign. It was an oppressive, one-hundred-degree day, uncomfortable as could be; a small town, glass-blowing and steel, and a typical campaign kind of circus. In the basement of a church the speech was given, and there was a cake in the shape of the White House. J.F.K. was in fine form, enjoying as always the people around him. He seemed to have boundless energy. This series, taken during a crucial campaign, went through as a blur of heat. All through this campaign there was the whirling on one side and the peaceful life in Georgetown on the other.

At the Virginia estate of Jacqueline Kennedy's mother, Mrs. Hugh D. Auchincloss.

Pages 55-61: Hyannis Port. The children growing up, surrounded by natural life, horses, sports, and travel.

Page 62: The twin-engine plane used for commuting between Boston and the Cape.

Pages 65-94: The John F. Kennedys at Hyannis Port. Typically the family was together, always celebrating birthdays, parties, anniversaries, conscious of outdoor life, the beach and the air. Most afternoons were spent along the water, walking, talking and playing with the children. Everyone would dress for dinner and gather in the living room. The talk would be on politics and the arts, and to be uninformed in that group was disaster. World history was attacked in the manner of an athletic contest. It was an adults' world after dark.

The inauguration gala started hours late because of the heavy snow. Less than half the guests were there at the beginning.

The White House nursery. The President, dressed to make a speech, stopped to play with John-John. Mrs. Maud Shaw, the proud nanny. Caroline, pleased to have her father there, kept playing around and finally the President scooped up John-John with a big hug and a little dance. Caroline thought of her brother as her personal doll. There was the same feeling as at Hyannis Port or Georgetown, except that this was the nursery on the top floor of the White House.

Page 104: Hyannis Port. Caroline being a photographer's assistant. John-John, his friend David Shaw, and Caroline all fighting over the buttered toast. The Kennedys start early to assert themselves.

Page 105 and following: The White House again. Caroline sneaking out from under the nursery bed to play with John-John and ending up taking my picture.

On the trampoline at Hyannis Port, full of enthusiasm and life.

The center hallway on the top floor of the White House, a sort of salon. At the far end was the Lincoln guest bedroom; the near end was used by the President and First Lady. On the left, a small private dining room.

The official photograph of John-John at one year, with Caroline and Jackie.

Caroline, the photographer's assistant, struggling to get John-John to stand. She carried the tripod and talked about my "yellow bird" airplane. She identified the plane with the photographs.

Pablo Casals. A most important night and Casals was like a small boy, happy and excited. There was a feverish air in the White House. When the concert was over and the President spoke, there was no other sound. It was a sparkling yet restrained evening. There was a small dinner for Casals and the musicians, who had not eaten before the performance, and everyone gathered around. The private dinner party lasted late into the evening.

Pages 130-133: The President's warning to a too-soft America to toughen up set off that craze, the fifty-mile walk. Everybody was doing it. After Robert Kennedy completed his speedy hike, the President's brother-in-law, Prince Radziwill, ended dinner one evening by saying he could do it. So began a test of physical and emotional determination. Agent Clint Hill, Charles (Chuck) Spalding, the President's roommate at Harvard, Stash Radziwill and others gaily started from quiet Palm Beach at one in the morning. It was typical of the enthusiasm for group projects. Friends loaded station wagons with steaks and fruit juice to follow the men down the Sunshine Parkway towards Miami.

All day the state troopers waved to the group, and tourists driving by looked over their shoulders in amazement.

Suddenly in the afternoon, without warning, the big white Lincoln rolled up, driven by the President. He had left his yacht to come and see how the group was faring. Various tender spots were displayed and Dr. Max Jacobson carefully checked the wounded extremities. He had been talked out of the hike after eleven miles when he turned his ankle. Stash was determined that the Polish banner would fly high, and Chuck that his Harvard class banner equally so.

Off and on during the day the First Lady, her sister Lee and agent Paul Landis brought some cheer to the weary hikers. By late afternoon, however, the gayness had worn off and a grim, determined group raced to try to keep up with Bob Kennedy's record time. The President was worried about Stash, but Dr. Max was on hand. It was difficult to keep Dr. Max from competing; as always, he was everybody's "good friend," and insisted on treating everyone in sight.

When darkness fell and the fifty miles were finally ours, all gathered at the Palm Beach White House for champagne and the President's "decorations"; inscribed tea bags in place of medals.

Page 134 and following: Palm Beach, the time of the announcement of the impending arrival of a third child. The dog Clipper playing in the water, John-John back of the house by the pool. John-John with a sense of humor and a twinkle in his eye. These were warm, happy times, with no feeling of the pressures that were to come.

Hyannis Port.

The President's office, November, 1963.

All of the photographs in this book, with the exception of the Casals series, were taken with a Nikon camera and Nikkor lenses.